Con

LIST OF ILLUSTRATIONS AND MAPS

SNOW ON THE EQUATOR

For Aoife
and
in memory of Niall and Diarmuid

Snow on the Equator

AN AFRICAN MEMOIR

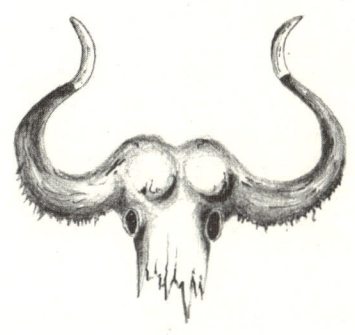

SEAN ROTHERY

ashfield
PRESS

Published in 2009 by
ASHFIELDPRESS • DUBLIN • IRELAND
© Sean Rothery, 2009
© Illustrations by Sean Rothery.

ISBN: 978-1-901658-77-4

This book is typeset by Ashfield Press
in 12.5 on 14.5 point Adobe Garamond
Designed by SUSAN WAINE
Printed in Ireland by COLOUR BOOKS LIMITED, DUBLIN

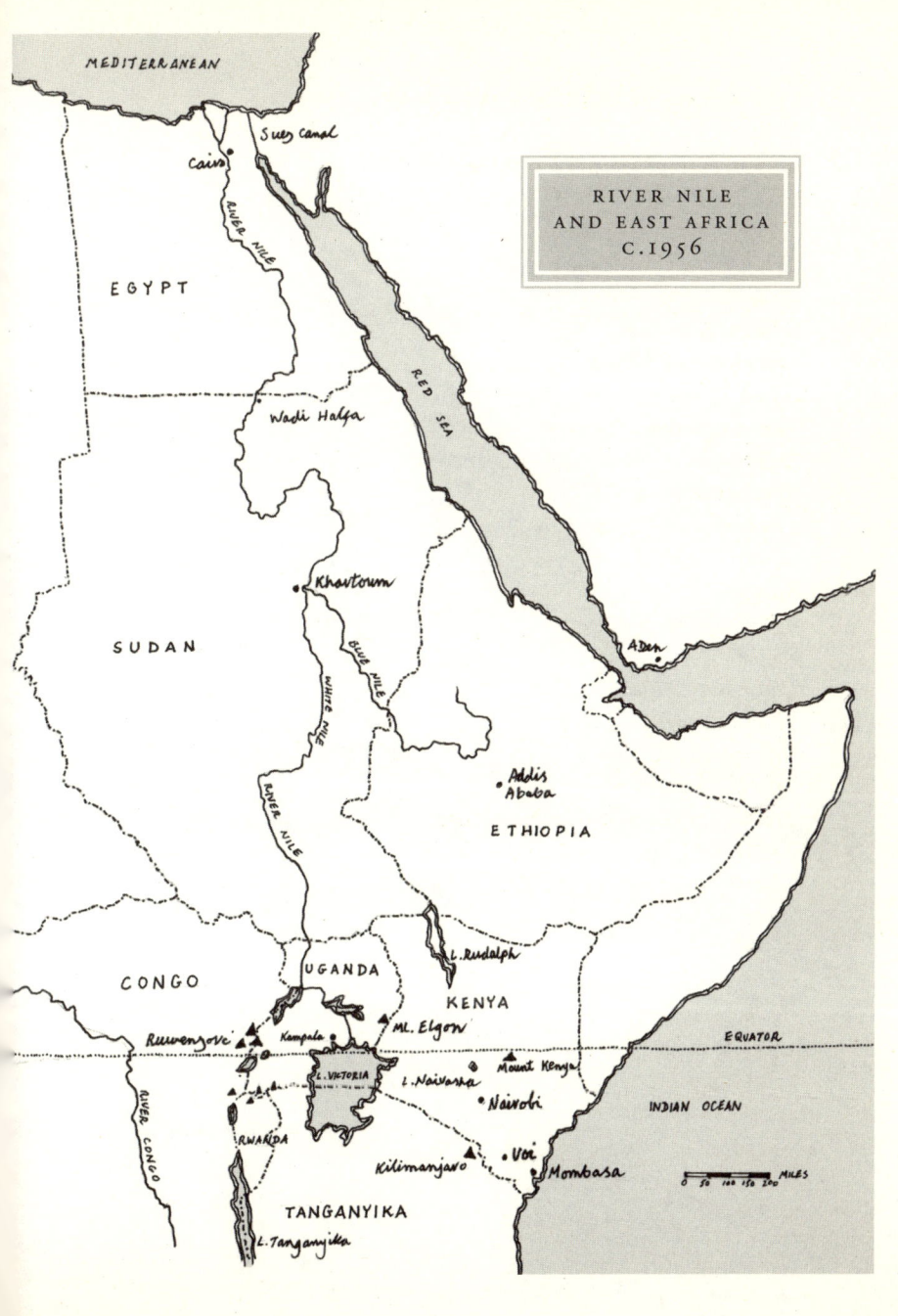

MEDITERRANEAN

Suez canal

Cairo

RIVER NILE
AND EAST AFRICA
C.1956

EGYPT

RIVER NILE

RED SEA

Wadi Halfa

Khartoum

Aden

SUDAN

BLUE NILE

WHITE NILE

Addis
Ababa

ETHIOPIA

RIVER NILE

L.Rudolph

CONGO

UGANDA

KENYA

EQUATOR

Ruwenzori

Kampala

Mt. Elgon

Mount Kenya

RIVER CONGO

L.VICTORIA

L.Naivasha

Nairobi

INDIAN OCEAN

RWANDA

Kilimanjaro

Voi

Mombasa

MILES

0 50 100 150 200

TANGANYIKA

L.Tanganyika

SUDAN

KENYA

CONGO

KARAMOJA

Imagit

RIVER NILE

× Murchison Falls

▲ Mt. Moroto

Moroto

L. Kyoga

▲ Soroti

L. Salisbury

Masindi

Nakasongola

▲ Kadam

L. Albert

Ruwenzori

▲ Fort Portal

Mbale

▲ Mt. Elgon

▲ Mount Speke

▲▲ Mount Baker

▲▲ Mount Stanley

Equator

Mityana

Kampala

Jinja

Eldoret

Entebbe

Mt. Bell

L. George

Kazinga Channel

L. Edward

Masaka

Mbarara

LAKE VICTORIA

▲ Kabale

▲ ▲ Muhavura

TANGANYIKA

RWANDA

Miles

0   30   60

UGANDA
C. 1956

ACKNOWLEDGEMENTS

FIRST THANKS must go to Nuala: the memories in this book are shared ones, sometimes divergent, but never very far apart and the story of this adventure is equally hers.

We went back to Uganda in 2006, fifty years after our first arrival there in 1956 as young innocents from a small island, eager for new experiences under the wide skies of Africa. The main purpose of our return was to rekindle memories of those early years, by revisiting places we imagined we would never see again.

Our return experience was greatly facilitated by Philip Curtin, the Managing Director of the Uganda firm of architects Peatfield and Bogdener. Philip had been a student at the Dublin School of Architecture and when he went out to Kampala after he graduated, he invited us to make a return visit sometime. The years of conflict in that beautiful country made us hesitate but eventually a tour organized by Naturetrek made for an enjoyable and valuable trip. Our particular thanks must go to Johnnie Kamugisha, a veritable encyclopaedia on the wildlife of that country, and to his assistant, Emmy. Philip entertained us at his splendid house at Gaba and gave us the services of his driver Fred for negotiating the appalling traffic of Kampala. We failed to find our old house on Mbuya, now a suburb instead of a green forest, but the cemetery on the Jinja Road was almost as we left it, an oasis of calm. We remember with fond appreciation the help of that lovely and dignified *mzee* who was responsible for the cemetery's upkeep and who helped us try to find those long-lost graves.

We appreciate also the support of Eoin and his partner Cath who travelled from Perth, Australia, to join us in Uganda and share the nostalgia of those early years.

Thanks also to Ian McPherson, Andrew Sharp and Carmel Habbington for their help in various ways and, finally, to John Davey, Susan Waine and Judith Elmes of Ashfield Press and Jonathan Williams for his inestimable editing skills.

CHAPTER I

INTO AFRICA

'Boy. *Laytay mawgee mautau*', said the man
in the deckchair.

H E WAS STRETCHED OUT, pinkish knees between
long white socks and shorts, on the terrace beside
the swimming pool. The young waiter, in the
uniform of white *kanzu*, green cummerbund and fez, looked
puzzled at the strangled Swahili vowel sounds but, since the
order was loudly repeated, smiled and answered in perfect
English, 'Ah, Bwana, *maji moto*, you need hot water for your
tea. I will fetch it at once, sir.'

'Welcome to Colonial Africa', we said to each other, even
though we had been there only a wet week, as they say at home.

It was 1956 at the exclusive Silver Springs Club on the
outskirts of Kampala, the capital of Uganda, part of British
East Africa. The swimming pool was for whites only or, as we
were sternly corrected by one of the long-term colonials,
'persons of European extraction'. Africans and Asians,
however, were allowed to buy drinks and sit on an upper
terrace beside the road and observe the privileged at play. It
was an early introduction to the rules of the game during
those last days of the British Empire in Africa.

Sunday, and the early morning sun was still a huge pleasure: later, the same sun would sear vertically overhead from an unbearably white sky where all blue was scorched. Behind us a screen of banana plants fringed a green mass of tall elephant grasses, while crimson and purple bougainvillea spilled out on to the poolside. After a cold northern winter, this new exotic tropical world was a visual shock, as well as a reminder that we had left our old life and all its certainties behind.

A year earlier Nuala and I had been perched on a high rocky ridge of the Cuillins on the island of Skye. We had just completed a long route up steep slabs: a climb that had started in sunshine and was a blissfully easy ascent on clean dry rock, but it had turned into a life and death struggle as a sudden storm sent torrents of water cascading down the overlapping slabs. The top of the ridge was finally reached as the rain passed. The pinnacles of the Cuillins poked up from the thick mists below and away to the east the grey sea stretched far to the mainland. We talked about our future together and where it would be. One thing was certain, however: it would be in some far off place, away from the bonds of family and home – an adventure perhaps, but most of all an escape.

Ireland in the early 1950s was a drab, dreary, church-dominated and uninspiring place. Foreign travel was for the rich and privileged; the real concern was finding a job, with emigration the only hope for many. The photographs of the time show a world in black and white, with all shades of grey in between: the belted rain-coated cinema queue shuffling towards the dream land of Hollywood was the temporary escape for many.

For our small group, however, there was another way to break out from this conformist, pietistic and stodgy milieu. The rounded green summits of the hills seen from Dublin's city's streets offered another way, another world. In 1946, my first-year study of architecture, I cajoled a reluctant fellow student to accompany me on a traverse of the Mourne Mountains, made in driving snow. Two years later Joss Lynam, just back from the Indian Army at the end of World War II, put an advertisement in a Dublin newspaper suggesting the formation of a climbing group. An enthusiastic meeting in a Dublin hotel founded the Irish Mountaineering Club, but I had first heard of it from Fred Maguire, another student in those decrepit architectural studios in the old university building in Earlsfort Terrace. I went out with Fred the following weekend and saw a party rock-climbing on the brooding crag over Luggala in County Wicklow. I was instantly hooked.

Weekends from then on were a dizzy joy. We still worked Saturday mornings but afterwards a motorbike ride took us into that other dimension. Here we could enjoy the sheer sensual pleasures of moving up a steep cliff and the fingertip texture of hard rock. The ultimate triumph was reaching the top, where we could stretch out in the heather, watching ravens swoop in the sky above. Cold winters in those years saw us cutting through snow cornices on the North Prison face of Lugnaquillia: a foretaste of the Alps and the delicious prospect of high peaks and glaciers; the intoxicating vernacular of mountaineering literature: *bergschrund, couloir, séracs, arête*, moraine, ice fall, crevasse, snow bridge, razor edge, *gendarme*, chimney, *brêche*. The Zillertal Alps in Austria first, then a season in that Mecca of climbing – Chamonix/Mont Blanc. A passion was born.

I met Nuala a few weeks after that punishing but exhilarating climbing adventure. It was at one of the mountaineering club's evening slide shows where new members were welcomed and where future liaisons often originated. I was immediately attracted to this long-legged twenty-year-old. Over the next few months we became close and were soon established as a couple in a disparate band of climbers who liked to see themselves as unconventional and even mavericks in the conformist society of the time. Every weekend we were walking in the hills or rock-climbing on the cliffs of Glendalough or Luggala and on summer evenings in Dalkey Quarry. The long weekends were precious, with epic camping trips to Connemara, Donegal, Kerry and the Mournes.

The 1950s were frustrating times for young architects. I was lucky in my first job after graduation. Michael Scott's office, on the beautiful eighteenth-century Merrion Square in Dublin, was certainly a most exciting place to be, in a society that was parochial, economically stagnant and downright dull. The 'Boss' was an extraordinary character – ebullient, charming and non-conformist – who allowed his staff to engage themselves in days of indulgently pretty design drawings, most never to be realized as buildings. Every architect wants to build, and gorgeous perspectives in ink and watercolour can never substitute for the real and solid structure rising into the light. The practice had one major project actually being built, but most of our dreams on paper seemed to wither and die.

I became increasingly restless in those early years. Little of

UPPER LAKE, GLENDALOUGH

my design work was actually built and sometimes what was completed ended up unrecognizable from my drawings. I think I must have reached a nadir with a pet project – a small petrol filling station to be located beside a nineteenth-century roadside house in the Midlands. This had a lovely old apple orchard on one side, and my idea was to locate the filling station on the other end, the ground floor of the house becoming a café, with a pergola extending into the orchard as open-air dining. The filling station was built, but on my next visit the orchard had been cut down and the space was concreted over. 'Client's orders', I was told.

Architecture and mountains – twin obsessions – but how to achieve satisfaction in both? The answer could only be in emigration, and starting to plan for this became a priority.

Sherpa Tensing and New Zealander Ed Hillary climbed Everest in 1953 and the then relatively small world of mountaineers was electrified. Everybody wanted to go to the Himalayas, but unfortunately few could afford the huge costs of an expedition like the successful British one. For me, architecture, however, offered a way to at least get close to those superb peaks. At the time, Le Corbusier was building his greatest project – Chandigarh – the new capital of the Punjab in India. There were few young architects who were not excited by the seductive drawings and photographs of this major work of modernism.

In our practice, the 'Corb' was king. A full-size Modular Man figure was painted on a wall in the drawing office and it was the rule that all measurements adhered to the proportions outlined there. The pioneering London firm of Maxwell Fry and Jane Drew became associates of Le Corbusier for the India project and I decided that approaching them for a job in Chandigarh might be more likely of success than going direct to the great man himself. I sent off a letter of application. For about two weeks there was no reply. Then one morning I got a call from the Boss wanting to see me in his office. He was his usual genial self, chatting about work, until he dropped the bombshell. 'My old friend Maxwell Fry tells

me that you want to leave us. Are you not happy here?'
Hardly knowing what to say, I told him that maybe I just
wanted to travel – see the world, have new experiences. He
assured me that I was a valued member of the team and that
there were new and exciting projects in the offing, but the
message was clear. He was not going to encourage me to go
and it was my first valuable lesson in the power of the old
boys' network.

From now on I realized that I would have to be more
discreet in my job-hunting. In the early 1950s the map of the
world still showed large chunks of red. The British Empire,
after India had achieved independence – and in politeness to
Australia, New Zealand and Canada, was now usually referred
to as the Commonwealth. The Colonial Office, however, was
still in business, and the architectural journals carried numerous advertisements with job offers in exotic-sounding places:
Malay States, Sarawak, Papua, Mauritius, Nyasaland,
Honduras, Hong Kong: some places were only little red dots.
I studied these avidly and tried to match the country with
serious mountain ranges.

I applied to one of these advertisements and promptly
received a reply asking me to attend for an interview at the
headquarters of the Colonial Office. I asked for a few days
off, not mentioning my plan, and travelled by boat and train
to London. The building was enormous but appeared to be
deserted. Long empty corridors floored in brown linoleum
led to a huge anti-room where the heavy oak wainscot seemed
forcibly to express the permanence and stability of the
Empire. I was the only person in this waiting area and was
beginning to wonder what the hell I doing there. Called into

the interview room, I was faced with three middle-aged men seated behind a long table. They each appeared to be dressed in identical brown suits, while the table held huge piles of manila folders. I expected the interview to have some reference to exotic places and refer particularly to the possible perils and problems facing intrepid young architects working in faraway jungles and deserts: restless natives, malaria, wild beasts and God knows what adventures. Instead, the talk was all about the importance of proper concrete mixes and firm foundations, careful measurements and accounting. I walked away, at the end, with a firm resolve that life in the service of government and its monochrome world was not for me.

From now on my search had to expand and explore more exciting areas of enterprise. Hailie Selassie, the Emperor of Ethiopia, intended building a massive new palace in Addis Abba. A design office was set up in that city and to work there became a most desirable aspiration for young designers. Unfortunately, many others had the same idea and, when I applied, there were no vacancies. Eventually I saw an advertisement from an international firm of architects with a chain of offices worldwide. This was a chance to take my pick of places, with big mountains of course, as well as attractive projects. My application received a prompt reply and a request to attend for interview to what I assumed was the firm's head office in Oxford. The club planned a climbing trip to the Ogwen valley in Snowdonia in North Wales and this presented a perfect opportunity to make a quick dash down to Oxford for the interview. We stayed in the Climbers Club hut near the base of the splendid Tryfan mountain, whose knife-edge rocky ridge seemed to slice the skyline. After the first day spent in the hills, I set off next morning, just after dawn, for the fast motorcycle trip south.

I somehow imagined that the headquarters of the great firm would be located near the core of this lovely city of honey-coloured spires and domes. Instead, the address brought me a long way out to the western suburbs until an iron gateway and nameplate announced the home of Brantwaithe and Partners, Architects. A short driveway, lined with evergreen oaks, led to a low sprawling bungalow, more in the style of a Victorian hunting lodge than the shining Modernist statement I eagerly anticipated. I rang the doorbell and an elderly housekeeper led me into a large gloomy hall to await my summons for interview. My heart sank as I glanced around the room. A pair of stag's antlers flanked a fireplace, with the centrepiece consisting of a glass case containing a stuffed fish. A few framed photographs and one large watercolour perspective drawing gave a flavour of the work of the firm. There was a bank building in Madras in Neo-Georgian; a hospital in Singapore with lots of round arches; a club house in Kingston, Jamaica, complete with heavy balustrading and corner minarets and, the final blow to my dreams of cutting-edge Modernism, a Gothic Revival church in Cape Town.

After a while, I was told that Mr. Brantwaithe would see me now and I was shown into a room where the firm's chief partner was seated behind a heavy walnut desk, with his back to a long window. He appeared old and he certainly did not fit my perception of how an eminent architect should look. The Corb's bow tie and black spectacles were the sorts of trademarks to be expected of those masters of Modernism we youngsters admired. This person looked so ordinary and the surroundings and furnishings so old-fashioned that I felt dejected and deflated. I expected to be questioned about my thoughts on architecture, my qualifications, and my knowledge of building science. Instead, I was treated to a eulogy about the firm, the breadth of its activities, the advantages the employees enjoyed and the size of the salary I could expect. I began to feel that Mr. B was the spider in the centre of a web hoping to catch naïve young architects for export to his vast empire of antediluvian monument-building.

The long ride back to Snowdonia was tedious and I felt depressed that my efforts so far at attempting to escape to a new life had failed, at least on my terms. By the time I arrived back to rejoin Nuala and the others, I had cheered up. A final sunny day high up on the fantastic tors of Glyder Fach cleared the memory of those sterile interviews and fossilized gentlemen in London and Oxford.

A bronze statue stands on the lawn outside the Museum of Natural History on Dublin's Merrion Square. The name inscribed on the high granite plinth is Surgeon Major T. H. Parke. The mustachioed figure stands tall, cross-belted, sleeves rolled up, with one booted foot resting on an animal skull. He leans on a long rifle and the pose is assured, confident, the very embodiment of the superior white man in Darkest Africa. The bronze plaque on the plinth is a vignette depicting an incident where the good doctor sucks the poison, inflicted by an arrow, from the body of a colleague during one of his expeditions through that continent in the late 1880s.

The story of Major Parke had interested me from the time

I first became aware of this statue. Dr Parke was a graduate of the Royal College of Surgeons in Dublin and his first adventure was to take part in the expedition for the relief of General Gordon in Khartoum. He was later chosen as physician to accompany Stanley on his famous expedition, his second crossing of Africa from coast to coast. It was on this trip, in 1888, that Parke, near Lake Albert in Uganda, saw the summit of a great snow-capped mountain emerging from the clouds. He thus became the first European to prove that the fabled 'Mountains of the Moon' existed. The ancient Greeks, as well as African legends, had long speculated that the source of the Nile lay in the heart of Africa, fed by great lakes and snow-covered mountains. Two days later, Parke told Stanley what he had seen. The expedition leader was at first scornful, but was later himself to claim credit for this discovery.

East Africa had been on the list of possible places to experience. I knew little about interesting opportunities there for young architects, but it certainly had mountains in abundance. The highest was Kilimanjaro in Tanganyika, but this was a stand-alone mountain, offering just a long uphill trudge and no serious mountaineering challenge. Mount Kenya was altogether more exciting: high, sharp rock peaks with many unclimbed routes in those days. The problem of Kenya was that the horrific Mau-Mau campaign was at its height and the area around the mountain range was under military control, with all access forbidden. That left the Ruwenzori, a great wilderness with snow-capped peaks and glaciers bordering Uganda and the Belgian Congo, some 60 miles long and 20 miles wide. Here was the most tempting prospect.

The Institute of Architects in London had a register where both job offers and applications could be posted. I submitted my name as being interested in work in East Africa and, a surprisingly short time later, a slim blue airmail letter arrived postmarked Kampala, Uganda. The stamp had an inset portrait of the young Queen Elizabeth II over a drawing of a lion standing under an acacia tree. The letter, from a firm of architects with offices in Kampala, Nairobi and Dar-es-Salaam, offered me a position in the head office in Kampala. The writer said that the practice was engaged in a wide variety of buildings: a General Post Office, a cinema, university buildings and shops, office blocks and housing. The salary offered was three times my present one and the firm would pay my airfare. The other conditions were, in hindsight, less positive, but my elation at the possible achievement of those twin goals of designs built and climbing in the 'Mountains of the Moon' was paramount.

Nuala and I had married two months earlier and our conviction as well as our optimism that we would soon be overseas and far away was reflected in the wedding presents from friends and relatives: travelling rugs, suitcases, a portable clock and – most importantly – money. I wrote back at once accepting the post, handed in my resignation, and the Boss, now generous in his encouragement of my decision to leave, threw us a big office party. The next few weeks were frenzied. We were advised to have as many household items as possible crated up and sent out by sea to Mombasa and then overland to Kampala. This operation could take at least four months. As newly weds, we had few possessions, so only a modest-sized wooden crate was sent on its long journey.

The next stage in our preparations was less pleasant: vaccinations and inoculations against smallpox, yellow fever, cholera, tetanus and typhoid were all mandatory. Fortunately, we had each had childhood vaccinations against smallpox, but the shots for the others left us nursing sore arms for at least a week. Malaria was the big problem in East Africa, so we were advised to stock up on anti-malarial tablets before we left. We read about other hazards, such as tsetse fly, which caused blindness, and horror stories about poisonous snakes surfaced from supposedly well-meaning friends when we announced our plans. The die was cast, however, and nothing could deter us from the coming adventure and our escape to a new life. A fresh letter arrived from Kampala with additional information, some positive and some less so. The firm would not pay Nuala's fare, but a loan from them could be paid back; a car was essential but this also could be a repayable loan; and, finally, the rent for a one-bedroom house would be 25 per cent of my salary. On the positive side, they said that Nuala could be offered employment and that for me an annual bonus would 'normally be paid'. We airily dismissed the negatives, the motorbike was sold, our tickets arrived, and the day of departure came.

Neither of us had ever flown. Air travel in the nineteen fifties was for the fairly wealthy and our journeys abroad always involved sea trips to Britain and the Continent. The crossing of the Irish Sea – three and a half hours to Holyhead or seven hours to Liverpool, was rarely a pleasurable experience. The ship for the longer journey often doubled as a cattle boat, where the smell of dung and the bellowing of the animals on their way to slaughter could conjoin the human passengers in misery. The shorter trip to Holyhead was often worse. The Mail Boat, as it was called, could sometimes be the venerable *Princess Maud*, known colloquially as the Vomit Maud. This had a tendency to roll like a porpoise and even almost rear upright when it met the first heavy swell after leaving harbour. To be airborne was a prospect for us to savour.

The first leg of our long flight took us into London, where we had to find our way out to a small building housing the romantic-sounding Hunting Clan Safari Air Service. The check-in was relaxed, and the twenty or so intending travellers, almost all European, sat around silently. After a long wait, we were told that the plane was ready and we were led out on to a field towards a huge, silver, four-engine Constellation aircraft. This is it I thought; only something so big can take us on the 4,000-mile journey. We marched under the wing of the monster and on the far side saw a tiny two-engine machine, sitting on its tail like a dog, waiting for us.

Heavy clouds over London and onwards over the English Channel eased to white puffy cumulus as we floated over northern France. The dark cloud shadows spotted the green landscape below and, since we were flying at only about 7,000 feet, every detail of the countryside was visible as a living map. As we edged farther south, I could see old walled towns, some perched on hilltops, in the Maritime Alps and then the intense blue of the Mediterranean slowly began to fill the panorama ahead.

We landed at Nice – for lunch, we were told, although the main reason was to refuel – a process to be repeated many times before we reached our destination. We took off into the afternoon sunshine from a runway parallel to the sparkling sea and turned slowly south. The next stop was Malta where we spent the night: our direction was then across the Mediterranean to Alexandria in Egypt and on down the Nile. This had been the route taken by the Imperial Airways flying boat service, started in 1936 and ended ten years later. I read that these graceful machines carried only 24 passengers or 16 in a sleeping berth layout. The passengers had a promenade deck to view the scenery at an altitude, sometimes, of only 1,500 feet. Waiters would serve champagne to these sybarites, who would loll on comfortable chairs and languidly gaze out at the world below. We were encased in a noisy little metal box, conversation was nearly impossible and our knees were jammed against the seats in front. To us it was still an adventure, however, and the sight of the islands of Malta, each with a white curl of surf, appearing out of the blue ocean in front lifted our spirits.

The Hotel Phoenicia in Valetta was another new experience: marble floors, a palm court, and a room with a balcony overlooking the Grand Harbour. We relished the delicious sensation of newness and fresh encounters, but that evening I was again aware of my anxiety about what lay ahead and of that nagging feeling of disquiet about cutting off old ties.

A splendid morning of glorious sunshine changed the mood. From our balcony we stared down at the famous harbour where smashed stonework was a reminder that Malta was one of the most bombed places in Europe during World War II. A further connection with those days was the presence of several naval vessels in battleship grey moored under the ramparts and stone bastions of the ancient forts.

In the air once more, the captain suddenly made an

GRAND HARBOUR, VALETTA

announcement that we would have to divert from our intended route. We would not be landing in Egypt, owing, he said, to 'political developments'. Before we left home the newspapers had been headlining an impending crisis in the relations between Britain and the newly installed nationalist leader of Egypt, Gamal Abdel Nasser. Until just a few years before, the British had occupied the zone of the Suez Canal with a huge military force, but they had reluctantly withdrawn their troops, leaving the canal to be managed by a British-controlled company – in effect the Suez Canal was still seen as a British possession.

Our destination was now Libya, and a place called El Benina, close to the Egyptian border. We flew for hours over the featureless Mediterranean, the sharp horizon ahead gradually softening into a horizontal smudge of beige, then slowly expanding until we drifted in over the long, low African coast-line. We landed on a barren strip of dusty plain and, when we clambered down the narrow steps, were surprised that it felt quite cool. Clouds of grayish dust were blowing and we were glad to reach the shelter of a corrugated iron shed where we were served sandwiches and cold drinks while the plane was refuelled. A couple of scrofulous palm trees outside and a rusty Shell petrol sign swinging in the wind were hardly the exciting first view of Africa for which we had hoped. The dust storm cleared as we boarded again and headed off over the Sahara: our new destination was Wadi Halfa, on the Nile and the northernmost border between the Sudan and Egypt.

I had brought with me a page from an old atlas and could see that a direct line to our next stop would take us across the Western Desert, skirting the Quatarra Depression but, unless we did an extraordinarily long dogleg, we had to cross a large chunk of Egyptian territory. I hoped Colonel Nasser would not object. For some time I had been watching an oil leak from the engine on my side growing larger as the hours went by. I debated whether or not I ought to tell the flight atten-dant, but decided that looking foolish if nothing was wrong was worse than the more remote possibility of crashing in the middle of the Sahara. The view below was fascinating: a yellow ochre landscape layered and folded with deeper saffron patches and now and then hillocks and rocky knolls punctu-ating the endless emptiness. When the first oasis appeared in the honey-coloured desert, it seemed shocking. In the clear air the sharpness of the acid green outline of the palms made an abrupt statement of lushness in the arid wilderness. For hour after hour we rolled on, lulled by the endless roar of the engines until even the view below palled in its unending progression to monotony. The captain's voice jolted us awake.

'We shall be landing in Wadi Halfa in fifteen minutes. You can see the Nile below on the starboard side.'

There it was, the great river, the longest in the world and the giver of life to one of the oldest civilizations in history. We flew in low and could see that the waterway was fringed with green: fertile fields and clumps of trees filtering out into the empty desert.

When the aircraft door opened and we stepped down, it was if we had walked into a furnace. The heat was terrifying. We had never experienced anything like it: our clothes felt heavy and unbearable; even breathing seemed difficult. It was worse, sweaty and smelly, in the rickety bus that bumped its way to the hotel. This was perched right on the riverbank and immediately offered a blessed shade from the burning sun. When we were shown to our room, our first thought was to fill the bath with cold water, strip off our heavy clothes and lie in the cool tub. Later in the evening the temperature dropped and before dinner we walked a short way along the river. The tall date palms were black against an evening sky turning violet and the waterway was dotted with the white triangular sails of feluccas beating their way upstream. It was a deeply romantic moment and we both had a sense of exultation that we were on a headlong rush to our new life and a fresh world of adventure.

The propeller fan in the ceiling of our room thumped all night, but did little to cool the fetid air. We were up just before dawn and on our way again as the sun rose quickly over the golden dunes to the east. The next leg of the flight was a relatively short one to Khartoum – where we would refuel for the last, very long, section to Entebbe. For several hours we followed the line of the Nile south as it traced a narrow jet-black streak carving through the barren landscape. My atlas described the area below as the Nubian Desert and, as we finally swung away from the river across the immensity of this empty waste, my thoughts went back to Surgeon Major Parke and his early African adventure. The very name Khartoum was loaded with evocations of heroism and derring-do, although for me, at least, the boyhood stories of A.E.W. Mason had much to do with it. Alexander Korda's great film of Mason's book *The Four Feathers*, for all its stiff upper lip jingoism and glorification of Empire, was escapist fantasy at its best. The film purported to tell the story of the campaign to revenge the death of Gordon at the hands of the 'Mad Mahdi'.

The relief expedition of 1885 had come up the Nile from Egypt and, when less than two hundred miles from Khartoum, the river makes a huge loop to the east, adding more than another two hundred miles to the waterway route. From the air I could visualize the long lines of troops in their stifling red uniforms and white helmets attempting to short-cut this loop over the savage terrain. Parke's experiences obviously did not diminish his enthusiasm for Africa because a few years later he was with Stanley on the gruelling struggle up the Congo towards Uganda and the Mountains of the Moon. My daydreaming helped to ease the monotony of the endless panorama of desolation below until, after a few hours, the river appeared again. The airstrip was on the outskirts of the old city of Khartoum, or Omdurman, to give it its Arabic name. Our only impression was of a jumble of low, dun-coloured buildings and small fields bordering the desert.

Refuelling took several hours while we sweltered in a blockwork shed that served as a terminal.

The last leg of the journey was the longest – some twelve hundred miles. Below us for much of the way was barren wilderness with nowhere to land until we reached Entebbe. The Blue Nile came out of the high mountains of Ethiopia and joined the main stream, the White Nile, at Khartoum: its principal source flowed from the northern shore of Lake Victoria, but it was fed also from Lake Albert and the glaciers of the Ruwenzori. Again we followed the long line of the river: an oddly reassuring landmark for our odyssey south. The uplands to the east were lost in a dark purple haze and when the river at last faded from view, we felt, on this the third day, that the flight might go on for ever. I think that we both must have slept because when we awoke the panorama ahead and below was a mosaic of intense greenery and grey-blue water – a lacework of forest and lakes. The horizon soon filled with the vastness of Lake Victoria and we flew low over the complex of bays, swamps and heavily wooded islands to land on the open, flat peninsula of Entebbe.

'I'm Alec Inglis.'

The stocky man, dressed in neatly pressed white shorts and open-necked shirt, introduced himself when we walked into the terminal building. He was the senior partner, but seemed a somewhat taciturn individual as he led us out to a waiting car. The sunshine was blinding, the air felt balmy, lush grassy slopes, fringed with palm trees, led down to the huge expanse of the lake: we were excited with the newness of everything, but apprehensive also of what lay ahead.

The drive into Kampala was a kaleidoscope of colour after a monochrome northern winter. The first surprise was the red earth and its almost violent contrast with the vivid greens of flamboyant vegetation. At times the roadway was hemmed in by high elephant grasses and dense forest, but now and then it changed to a great table-flat sweep of tall papyrus where the lake edges turned to swamps. In some places the thick growth was cut away for small plantations of banana plants and little traditional huts of red clay smeared over timber wattles, each roofed with fronds of palm and grasses. Inglis said very little except that we would be staying in a hotel until our house was ready. We were too overawed by the sheer strangeness to ask him any serious questions.

The forest thinned on the outskirts of Kampala and we could see the first of the low hills where the city was located. Fresh greenery now gave way to a roadside lined with huts, surrounded by beaten and barren earth, with the traditional buildings morphing into tin-roofed shacks. In the gaps we could see a chaotic jumble of flimsy dwellings spreading out to fill the valleys, while red-roofed bungalows dotted the slopes. The main hill, called Kololo, soon dominated and, to my relief, this had large, solid modern buildings, giving me hope of exciting work to come.

It seemed entirely appropriate that we were to stay at the Speke Hotel. My thoughts on the long journey out had been dominated by those audacious explorers of the nineteenth century and who more famous than John Hanning Speke, the discoverer of the source of the Nile, only a few miles from where we now were? It was only later that we found out that the hotel was known locally as 'The Unspeakable' and that we should have been housed at the more posh Imperial.

A posse of porters, dressed in long white robes, met us at the entrance and took our bags to our room.

Our first night in Uganda was a revelation. Instead of the slow descent from twilight that we were used too, the day seemed to crash violently into darkness – the equatorial twelve-hour day and twelve-hour night would now be, for us, the unchanging norm. After dinner we went out for a short walk and a tentative exploration of this new world. Strange sounds and smells at once assailed us. A cacophony of weird croaks, caws, screeches, whistles, churring and burbling cadences from hidden birds and animals in the trees and bushes filled the night. Later, in our stuffy room, the bed encased in an enormous mosquito net hung from the ceiling, the incessant noise of cicadas would lull us into sleep.

FELUCCA, RIVER NILE

CHAPTER 2

OUR HOUSE ON MBUYA

'The first thing you have got to remember is that these
bastards are just down off the trees.'

THIS VERDICT on the six million black population
of an ancient kingdom was delivered by a small
dapper figure dressed in sharply pressed khaki shorts
and shirt. He said his name was Sergeant Major Cole and he
had the kind of reddish angry face and pinched moustache
that seemed appropriate to his title.

We were at the old abandoned airstrip on top of Kololo
hill, waiting for a driving lesson or at least for a refresher
before we took the essential driving test for our Uganda
licence. On our first morning in Kampala we were faced with
a bewildering list of tasks. The first was to acquire a car: we
could not, we were told, survive without one. The office had
already bought one for us – a little Fiat 600, with the wonderfully evocative number plate UFO 782. It was second-hand
and the cost was to be deducted monthly from my salary. It
was our first car and we were delighted with it, not yet realiz-
ing the state of Uganda's roads outside the capital. The
Sergeant Major was efficient as a teacher, so much so that after
just two hours we both took our tests. I had years of motor-

cycle experience, although less in cars, but Nuala had never driven a car and had piloted my motorbike only once or twice. We both passed first time, despite Nuala being made to drive through a crowded and chaotic market.

The second partner of the architectural firm was Bill McGuinness, a handsome man who always wore an elegant light linen suit and long trousers, instead of the commomplace shorts of the expatriate white males. The third partner, Frederick Wilkinson, was based in Dar-es-Salaam and all three had been servicemen in the Royal Air Force, but, unlike our Sergeant Major, they did not continue to use their service ranks. This practice seemed to be peculiar to white Kenyans, we were told. Many of these had come to East Africa as settlers and their sense of superiority could be reinforced by the military title. Kenya, our informant said, was awash with Squadron Leaders and Wing Commanders. There was a story that a demobbed Cockney mechanic in Nairobi was so incensed at the number of Captains, Majors and Colonels who came to his garage that he put up his nameboard as 'Private Smith'.

In the days ahead we were to encounter many more comments similar to the one from our driving instructor. Everyday casual remarks revealed deep prejudices and stereotyping that occasionally exposed rank intolerance. All this was new to us, but we were now part of Colonial Africa and soon would learn to cope and even enjoy challenging the xenophobia and downright ignorance displayed of the history and culture of the 'Dark Continent'.

Our new house was on a green hill called Mbuya, just outside the eastern boundary of the city. We were eager to see

OUR HOUSE ON MBUYA

it and set off down the Jinja Road, past the white Kibuli mosque, a prominent landmark perched on another of the hills of Kampala, and entered the forest that surrounded the city. This was one of the few tarmac stretches of road in the country and it continued down the route to Port Bell, a ferry port on Lake Victoria, where we were directed to find a turn-off opposite the Silver Springs Swimming Club. This couldn't be it, we said, as we stared at what resembled a dry riverbed leading straight up the hill. The red murram track was heavily channeled, incredibly potholed and the deep ditches on each side were an ominous testimony to occasional horrendous rainfall. I revved the little Fiat and bumped up in first gear, zigzagging to avoid the deeper holes, until the steepness eased and the track led out into a large open space cleared of bushy vegetation.

Six identical little houses, spaced asymmetrically, were set well apart from each other and sited on a slope to the south. Low-pitched, red-tiled roofs sat on white plastered walls, with the first three feet above ground level painted a deep terracotta. We recognized this feature of concrete buildings as another sign of the effect heavy rain could have when it splashed on the red earth, staining the walls. Our house was the highest up the hillside, with four steps leading to a veranda, deeply shaded by a wide roof overhang. A glazed steel door led into the living room and the single bedroom opened off this. At the rear, a tiny kitchen and a small bathroom completed the space, but it was our first home and we loved it. High trees below the slope obscured the view, but there was a reassuringly cosy feel to the little group of houses: the clearing transformed into an enclosure formed by tall elephant grass and dense forest. It was peaceful there, with only birdcalls and the sound of distant voices. Several pawpaw trees and banana plants shaded the undeveloped garden and the ground looked rich enough to make anything grow. There was much to do, however, before we could move in.

The first problem to be solved was furniture and the second was staff. The first was obviously essential but the second we queried: 'Do we really have to have servants?' The office secretary was horrified. She had been given the job of advising us on settling in. 'You must have at least one houseboy for cooking and cleaning and you must also have a shamba boy to do the garden and to clear around the outside. Nobody can manage without servants; it just isn't done out here', she said sniffily.

We began the hunt for furniture, determined not to get into further debt. The handful of furniture stores in the city had little but heavy Government Issue horrors of heavy chairs and settees in dark wood and liver-coloured leather. Eventually we found a small shop offering simple basket easy chairs that not alone suited our modern minimalist taste, but were also cheap and comfortable for such a hot climate. The bed was easy to solve, we were told. The roadsides near the city were lined with little shacks and huts with outdoor workshops making chairs, tables, stools, shelves and beds. The idea was that you bought a mattress in one of the city stores and had the base and frame made up on the spot. We agreed a price from a smiling, eager, old man or *mzee* – a respectful term, we were told, because an elderly person was valued and admired.

'It will be ready in two hours', he said confidently, shouting orders to his two very young assistants. When we returned at the appointed time, the bed was ready. The legs and frame were made from podocarpus, the ubiquitous everyday wood for building in Uganda, while the base consisted of a heavy wire mesh stretched tightly over the frame. This simple if crude system had the virtue of being cheap but, more importantly, considering the hot humid climate, it ensured that the underside of the mattress was aired. A more alarming admonition was to watch out for bugs and insect life of all sorts which could be drawn to warm beds. *Dudus*, as they were called in Swahili, often featured in horror stories told to newcomers.

During these first days I had to combine all the problems of house organizing with settling in to work in the office. A job had been lined up for Nuala in the Department of Education, which was conveniently next door to my architectural firm. We were both, therefore, working flat out almost from our arrival. Everything felt new and exciting, however, and we revelled in the hectic activity, the dawn to dusk sunshine and the sheer pleasure of building a home together. The mattress was roped to the roof of the Fiat that evening and when we stopped at the workshop, the base was ready. What seemed like an army of helpers tied it on top of the mattress and we inched slowly up our track, the potholes now near mastered by careful swerving, followed by numerous stops and starts.

Word had gone out that servant jobs were available. We had hardly unloaded the bed before a polite African approached, introducing himself as Peter. He was about forty, dressed in clean but tattered dark blue shorts and shirt. He handed over his references and waited respectfully while Nuala read them. The papers described him as hardworking, honest and reliable and, since neither of us had ever had anything to do with servants, let alone hiring anybody, we at once gave him the job. He moved into the little concrete one-roomed house in the rear garden, which our newly acquired white acquaintances grandiloquently referred to as 'the servants' quarters'. Peter solemnly informed us the next morning that since he would now be expected to wait at table when we entertained guests, he would have to be properly dressed. It came as a bombshell, especially to Nuala, that entertaining people with our meagre possessions might soon be on the agenda and especially with our crate from Ireland not due to arrive for months. With our new 'houseboy' perched on the rear seat, we drove back into the city and the African Clothing Store where Peter was fitted out with a long white *kanzu*. He beamed with pride in his new uniform and we realized the importance of having a job and the status it gave. The office secretary had warned us not to pay above the going rate for servants. 'This would spoil it for the rest of us and, in any case, they are mostly lazy and unreliable and not worth any more than the minimum.'

The minimum she suggested sounded ridiculously low, so we added a little which made us, at least, feel more comfortable.

The 'shamba boy' – gardener – to us was an altogether different necessity, but a no less important one. The problem was mosquitoes. Malaria was the deadliest of a long list of diseases in Africa, killing more people than all the others put together. The British Colonial Government had to be given the credit for introducing strict and sometimes draconian regulations to control the menace of the mosquito. The first edict was that no standing water was tolerated. This meant no gutters, downpipes or narrow drains where water could lodge and provide breeding ponds for the insects. The second important regulation was that all tall grass had to be cut regularly so that there were no damp areas near any building. The shamba boy's main task was to cut the grass every day or two and keep the wide, open drains free of debris and allow rainwater to clear away quickly.

Our next-door neighbour was a morose individual: a recent arrival from Killiney, south of Dublin, who worked as a solicitor in the Attorney General's office. He approached us in a somewhat diffident manner, suggesting that we share his shamba boy because there was hardly enough work in one of these small plots. We agreed and he walked off without further conversation. We thus acquired half of a second servant. Peter was already calling Nuala 'Memsahib' and me 'Bwana', so we ruefully wondered if we were to be so quickly absorbed into the colonial set. The truth of the matter was that, in those days, all that was required was to be white: it was axiomatic that a sense of superiority and the arrogance that goes with it depended on the colour of one's skin. In the days to come, however, we made new friends, began to absorb some of the fascinating history and culture of this ancient land and to appreciate a different world to the narrow closed one of the settler, colonial and expatriate.

The first explorers, men like Speke, Burton, Stanley, Grant, Murchison and the arch imperialist Captain Lugard, were each celebrated in eponymous place-names, thus reinforcing the belief that Uganda's history began with these intrepid Europeans who brought civilization to 'Darkest Africa'. The fact was that cultivators had settled the fertile African Rift Valley from at least the 4th century BC. Bantu-speaking people then established clan-based kingdoms and governments, leading to whole states being formed by the first millennium AD. The majority of white ex-pats, whose attitudes to the majority population ranged from benevolent patronage to downright contempt, knew little of this history. One of our new friends, Valerie Vowles, who ran the tiny Uganda Museum in Kampala, helped to educate us in this wider view of African history. She in turn introduced us to Alan Warner, Professor of English at Makerere University. Alan was something of a white refugee from the soon to be imposed apartheid system in South Africa. He had worked in the racially tolerant Fort Hare University, in the Eastern Cape Province, until it was taken over by the National Party Government, which promptly expelled all the liberal staff.

We had arrived in Uganda at a time of looming change. Kampala, although the capital of Uganda, was the centre of the important kingdom of Buganda; the head of this one-time separate state was known as the Kabaka. The present king was Edward Mutesa II, whose full name was the impressive-sounding Sir Edward Frederick William David Walugembe Mutebi Luwangula Mutesa. His supporters in the Buganda region knew him as King Freddy. The Kabaka was the latest in a long line of royal rulers of Buganda dating back to the fourteenth century. Henry Stanley described visiting the royal palace at Mengo in 1875, to find an impressive compound, set on top of a hill, comprising huge grass-roofed buildings and surrounded by a wall more than four miles in circumference.

Uganda had a disturbed and bloody history in the decades after the first explorers arrived and opened the way for colonization by European powers. After the Great War the Germans lost their colony of Tanganyika and the whole of East Africa came under the control of the British. It was the climax of the Empire. Kenya became a colony, with large numbers of British settlers arriving to take the best land for farming. Uganda, on the other hand, was described as a Protectorate, with a limited amount of self-government allowed to local chiefs and kingdoms, particularly Buganda.

When India achieved independence in 1947, the end of the British Empire was in sight. The rise of nationalism in West Africa, particularly in the Gold Coast, stirred the Colonial Office in London to prepare for the eventual independence of the African possessions. A new Governor of Uganda, Sir Andrew Cohen, arrived in 1952 and set about preparing the country for independence. His first act was to reform the Legislative Council, which was weighted in favour of the European community. He took in African representatives elected from districts throughout Uganda, but this brought him into conflict with the leaders of the kingdoms, particularly the Baganda people. The main bone of contention was that the British wanted a federation of the three East African territories – Kenya, Uganda and Tanganyika – but Ugandans wanted none of this. The white supremacist settlers of Kenya, in a country mired in the terrible Mau Mau uprising, which began in 1950, could dominate in any such federation, as Ugandan Africans could see happening in Rhodesia with the newly formed Federation of Rhodesia and Nyasaland.

The Baganda, however, also felt threatened by the possibility of the formation of a large nation-state. This could inevitably damage Buganda's self-interest and its belief in its own feeling of superiority in a region of diverse cultures and economic wealth. The Kabaka was persuaded by his subjects to refuse to co-operate with the plan for all-Uganda elections and he was promptly deposed by the Governor and deported to exile in London. It was a typically British miscalculation – the creation of a martyr. The Baganda were enraged, no one would co-operate with the central administration and, in

1954, as a protest, the famous drums of the King's palace were ordered to be silent until the Kabaka was allowed to return. After two years, Governor Cohen relented and King Freddy came back to his palace on Mengo's green hill. When we arrived some months after this, the country had entered a period of relative calm.

'No no, memsahib. The book – read the book.'

Peter had elected himself as tutor to Nuala as she began to master Swahili, the common language of East Africa. It was a Swahili-English dictionary and, although our new house-boy was perfectly fluent in English, he thought it his duty to teach Nuala this widely spoken African language. Some grasp of Swahili was necessary in everyday dealings in shops, markets, work and, above all, when travelling anywhere in the wider country. Nuala quickly became quite fluent in the language and, as a result of conversations with Peter, learnt something about his family and life in his village. Appreciation of African customs was almost non-existent for the majority of the white ex-pats we encountered every day. Once in Nuala's first weeks of work she was chatting to an African staff member, and addressed him by name. This seemed to amaze a fellow worker who said 'I can't tell them apart. How do you do it?'

In those first weeks we were quickly educated in the essential hierarchy of colonial society. On top were the whites; the politer synonym was 'European'. There were just 5,000 of us in Uganda. Next came the Asian population, which at 50,000 were the dominant business community. Last were the six million Africans.

The most visible way that this hierarchy was manifest was in the provision of lavatories. Every public building had toilets labelled 'European', 'Asian', and 'African'. The subdivision into male and female meant that there were usually six sets of such essential amenities to be catered for in each new building design. 'The battle of the jakes', an architect colleague called it, as I struggled to fit what looked like a forest of WCs into a project for a new bank.

The composition of the architectural practice was a microcosm of the larger society in Uganda. The architects were the two partners, Alec Inglis and Bill McGuinness; the senior assistant and myself the Europeans. The two draughtsmen were Asian, while our only African staff, apart from a cleaner who doubled as a messenger, consisted of two youths employed as apprentice draughtsmen. Our secretary and front office receptionist was South African and therefore qualified as 'European'. This pyramidal structure was ostensibly based on class or culture, as we were so often sternly rebuked when we mentioned race. 'They have different hygienic habits, eat spicier food, and sweat more than us, you know.' This was the excuse for 'whites only' swimming pools and clubs in a society where there was certainly a far less overt colour bar than in Kenya or South Africa, but the separation was there, unstated but emphatic.

The practice occupied the ground floor of a banal modern office block, situated on the lower slopes of Kololo hill. The street was named after James Grant, another one of the early European explorers of Africa. Having his name given to this architectural assemblage of identical concrete cubes would hardly have impressed Grant, who was with the expedition when Speke discovered the source of the Nile in 1858. The glorious jacaranda trees, however, which lined many of Kampala's roadways, splendidly softened the repetitious façades and, in season, the cloudy blue blossoms were a huge pleasure as we drove to work.

The office reception was the domain of the formidable secretary, undeviatingly referred to as Mrs. Caffrey. I never heard her addressed by her first name. She was a white South African, and a more typical stereotype of that colour-prejudiced society would be hard to imagine. She treated African and Asian staff, and visitors too, with a cold curtness bordering on contempt. The partners, two very different individuals, occupied the front offices. Alec Inglis was older, imperturbable and meticulous in the day-to-day affairs of a very busy practice, but was often somewhat remote. Bill McGuinness was the opposite – ebullient, amicable and always available for advice or suggestions over the drawing board. The senior assistant was Alan Pratt, a tall Englishman some five years my senior. He, to my surprise, told me had come from Addis Abba, where he had been one of the eager young designers recruited to build the Emperor of Ethiopia's great palace. The project had stalled and most of the foreign architects had lost their jobs. Kampala offered a refuge since it was then in the early stages of a building boom. Alan's office was a small separate space off the main drawing office where I was now installed.

My colleagues in this large bright space were the two African apprentices and the two Asians. Pius Kiyuima was a Mugandan:

a young man with a sunny disposition, eager to learn. His much younger friend, John, was extremely shy and always seemed in awe of his surroundings. Both Asians were Sikhs, as were most of the people in the building industry. Gurvinder Singh was an older man, with many years experience in architectural practice, and a fastidious worker whose punctuality could put us all to shame. He had come on contract from Bombay. He told me that his wife and children were still there and that he sent most of his earnings back for their support. Mohinder Singh Chana was a completely different character. He wore the most perfectly tied turbans, swooping up to a sharp point in front. He usually had a jewel or shiny stone centred exactly above his forehead. His beard was jet black and he spent a lot of time stroking it as he stared out of the window. He was usually late and Gurvinder did not approve.

A few weeks after I started work, a new staff member arrived from Europe and joined me in the drawing office. Walter Ryder was a building surveyor from Aberdeen whose job was to act as a supervisor of the increasing number of projects now moving off the drawing boards and rising out of the ground. Walter was a cheerful and adventurous Scot who could not wait to experience his new life in Africa. As a sixteen-year-old he had been in the Merchant Navy and had taken part in the invasion of France in 1944. In the tradition of the old Empire in India, which was mirrored in British Colonial Africa, Walter, as a single man, was installed in the Bachelors' Quarters of the East Africa Company. As incomers to this strange new world, we felt drawn together and, with Nuala, quickly became firm friends.

It was a strange world: in effect, it was split into three

worlds – white, brown and black, and initially at least, friend-ships and acquaintances tended to be forged almost exclusively within one colour group. Jean Jonnes was a colleague of Nuala in the Department of Education and she and her husband, Philip, were the first like-minded couple we befriended. We were much the same age and had similar enthusiasms. Jean was a petite Englishwoman with a great sense of humour, and Philip, an Australian, was a lover of the outdoors – and cars. He was an engineer with the international construction firm Mowlem which had just begun a programme of road-building in Uganda. Jean was a considerable mimic and often teased Philip about Aussie accents and foibles. She told us a story about one lady who, describing life in the outback, said that they were able to cope with the heat as 'some people have refrigerators and some have oice chists'.

On the other side of the coin we met some whose attitude to colour and race were shocking, often inviting confronta-tion. An early introduction to this was an invitation to dinner with the formidable Mrs. Caffrey, whose views on Africans and Asians we were well aware of, and her husband Jim, who had emigrated to South Africa from County Tyrone. Before we sat down to be waited on by their houseboy, Jim produced a bottle of whisky. Pulling out the cork, he threw it over his shoulder. 'This is the way we do things in Africa', he said. 'The bottle must always be finished before the night is out.' He then regaled us with tales of his adventures at work where he was a supervisor on the Ugandan railways. He was a big, powerfully built man and he described how he quelled trouble from his work gangs by carrying a policeman's truncheon in his hip pocket.

The City Bar was one of the few social meeting places in Kampala in those days. A restaurant with a wide veranda for outdoor lounging was a favourite hang-out for the expatriate population – a code name for whites. It was pleasurably exotic to sit on this shady terrace with the fronds of banana plants and bamboo cutting out the glare of the noonday sun while drinking a glass of the locally brewed Bell beer. I had my first experience of Indian cuisine here. I choose a curry and they said that it had been made cooler, to suit a European taste. Unfortunately, what I took to be green beans on the plate – I enthusiastically munched a large mouthful – turned out to be chillies. My mouth burned for hours.

At lunchtime one day Nuala and I were sitting with a new acquaintance. 'I am an old Africa hand,' he said, regaling us with tales of his exploits in the bush or 'on safari', as such old hands described any journey outside the city limits. In the middle of a conversation he suddenly exploded. 'Would you look at that bastard?' We could only see a neatly dressed African strolling by and wondered what was the matter. 'He's wearing a collar and tie', he explained. As newcomers, we needed to be educated.

We could encounter these violently opposing attitudes to race and colour almost daily, but soon learned when to ignore and when to confront. However, it was more comfortable to disregard the intolerance and ignorance and enjoy the company of the increasing number of people we met who could immerse themselves in the diverse culture and happy-go-lucky vitality of this exciting place.

The most exclusive establishment in Kampala was the Top Club. It was one of those cliquish associations that were restricted to 'whites only', modelled on those gentlemen's clubs of London and indeed of Dublin. The partners suggested to Walter and me that we might like to join. The unspoken sentiment was that it would be good for business and, anyway, it was 'the done thing'. The India Raj was never far away, although the East Africa version of it was definitely at a more plebeian level. We never did get round to joining since neither of us could envisage ourselves as members and we couldn't afford the subscription, considering our debts to the practice.

Our lives settled into a pattern in the weeks after we had established ourselves in the little house on Mbuya. It was a pattern very different to the one we had grown into back home. We were a mere twenty-five miles north of the Equator and had equal day and night all year. The altitude of Uganda was just over four thousand feet, so the temperature seldom varied by more than a few degrees throughout the year. In short, we were enjoying an almost perfect climate. Gone were the raincoats and greatcoats, along with heavy woollens and dark suits. The European men almost invariably wore shorts and light-coloured shirts. Shorts were white or khaki: white was sometimes preferred for Sundays. The houseboy, or a second servant if you had been in government service in Kenya or India, hand-washed clothes daily and whites were always sparkling and shorts ironed shiny smooth. European women wore skirts or summer dresses, and the saris of Asian women were an explosion of gaudy colour in the streets. Many African women wore the traditional dress: a voluminous gown, strongly patterned with puffed-out sleeves and bustles. Most African men wore often-tattered *kanzus* or shorts and a shirt. On Sundays it was notable how everybody wore their best for church: crisp and dazzling white shirts and blouses predominated.

Peter arrived in the kitchen just after dawn and had the breakfast laid out for us: delicious, juicy pawpaw, plucked from one of the trees in our garden, followed by tea and toast. The sun rose, day after day, inevitably into a clear blue sky, but had not yet cleared the tops of the tall trees surrounding our clearing as we set off to work. We became experts now at negotiating the rough track down to the Port Bell Road while the drive into the city was fast and easy, with little traffic. Out of the forest onto the main road to the city, the trees thinned and the first tin-roofed shops appeared with lines of men and women walking in single file, some carrying loads balanced on their heads as they strode along, upright and assured. Bicycles were used for even more spectacular balancing acts. Monstrous piles of *matoke*, the green bananas that were the staple diet of Ugandans, were heaped up, held in place seemingly by faith or maybe by expert selection, and then the whole cargo was laboriously pushed and wheeled towards the main city market. Bundles of sugar cane, making unbelievably wide loads, were tied across the rear carriers and these were hazards to be avoided because some mad cyclists weaved and wobbled to avoid the potholes.

The white Kibuli Mosque, with its twin minarets and dome, perched high on one of the hills, signalled the start of the city. Kampala to us in those early days seemed to be a paradise garden of tropical colour, from the yellow of the flowering acacias and the blue of the jacarandas to the cascades of purple bougainvillea and the shocking scarlet bloom of hibiscus. This idyllic picture was marred when we passed the municipal rubbish dump, where a line of repulsive black vultures lined up on the fence, waiting for each new consignment.

Our workday usually ended at 4 o'clock, which left little time for outdoor activity before the long nights, but our forest enabled us to take a cool walk after the burning sun of the day. Tracks led out through the tall elephant grass past small clearings, with little *shambas* of banana plants and round red huts down to the swamps bordering the lake. Large ditches had been cut here for drainage and a forest of eucalyptus trees had been planted many years before. The edges of the ditches offered a dry pathway and we soon found an agreeable circular route through the tall red pillars with their peeling barks and air filled with the strong scent of the resinous leaves. Before darkness fell, we often heard the sound of distant drums and singing voices from the direction of the lake. We asked Peter one evening who was doing the singing.

'They are the prisoners', he replied. 'They are trying to be happy.'

We accepted this somewhat benign observation on the soon to be notorious prison at Port Bell.

Before dark, it was Peter's ritual to close doors and window louvres before spraying a noxious-smelling insecticide around all openings, curtains, ceiling corners, under the bed and anywhere *dudus* could hide or, particularly, mosquitoes could enter. Later we could open the vents to air the rooms, although little breeze could fan past the close mesh of the wire screens. Before bed, however, it was tempting to

KIBULI MOSQUE

spend a little time out on the veranda, drinking a cold beer and listening to the still strange sounds of the African night, the sky above an infinity of blackness and a myriad of stars.

CHAPTER 3

BUILDING BONANZA

'We just blew one of their gunboats out of the water.'

BILL MCGUINNESS burst into the office one morning with the news.

'We've invaded Egypt. We're taking back the Canal!'

It was only a couple of months since we had arrived in Uganda and during that period the papers had been debating the growing dispute between Colonel Nasser and the British government over the Suez Canal, which Nasser had dramatically declared was now the property of Egypt. The office buzzed with the story: the ex-servicemen reliving their war years; even the Scot, Walter, was joining in the flag-waving. The Asians remained impassive, the young Ugandans smiled politely and I did my best to stay aloof from the rejoicing. In October 1956 the Israeli army invaded Egypt, pushing across the Sinai Desert to the east bank of the canal, then a few days later the British went in by air and sea to take control of Port Said and then drive south to seize the waterway. For the first few days the talk was about the possibility of the invasion of Egypt from the south, through British-controlled Sudan.

'We could all be conscripted, including you', Bill said to me, half in jest I hoped. The Sunday papers usually arrived a week after publication and it soon became evident that some of the press, particularly *The Observer*, were vehemently opposed to this adventure. The international disapproval was even greater and, after just a few weeks, the Americans forced a ceasefire and a British withdrawal. The Canal was now closed by the bombing and by ships sunk in the waterway. After an initial burst of jingoistic diatribes – 'the Gippos will never be able to manage the Canal' – the outcry died down. The humiliating defeat of Suez caused the fall of Sir Anthony Eden and was another pointer to the end of imperialism.

Of more immediate concern to the expatriates in East Africa was the loss, as they saw it, of their lifeline to the homelands. The great majority of trips to Britain for home leave, for instance, were by ship. These would now have to be re-routed, involving a huge detour around the west coast of Africa, past the Cape and back up the Indian Ocean to Dar-es-Salaam and Mombasa. The worry now was: would this extra time on the voyage come out of their home leave? In less than a year, however, the Canal, under Egyptian management, was functioning efficiently and effectively again and the whole affair was forgotten in the African colonies.

My early days in the office were a revelation. After such a sterile period back home, where nothing seemed to be built, here it was the opposite: a huge building programme and enticingly diverse projects. To a young architect, this was heaven, particularly the astonishing realization that when the design drawings were barely complete, the building could start. My first project was a house for the headmaster of a new Muslim school associated with the local mosque. I learned here some basic rules of design in tropical Africa. The first was that, while rising damp was not a problem, climbing ants or termites were a serious one. All domestic buildings had ant-proof courses and every house had to be inspected regularly for these insects. They had to be prevented from climbing through the walls and creating red mud tunnels up the outside of the building to reach the highly desirable roof timbers. The next task was to design a multi-functional window. This had to let in light, provide ventilation, keep out mosquitoes and, last but by no means least, it had to deter burglars. Every house had mesh screens and burglar bars or metal grilles. Even these did not deter the determined thief because fishing rods could be inserted past the grilles and through the mesh to pluck out carelessly left wallets or jewellery. Designing for petty crime was an essential element of every project and the burglar bars and grilles were usually made up at one of the outdoor roadside workshops.

We had a dramatic example of the way African rough justice could be inflicted on thieves one Saturday morning when we made our regular visit to the big city market for fresh fruit and vegetables. A commotion started near a stall we were inspecting: a noisy crowd gathered around a man on the ground who, to our horror, was apparently being beaten to death with concrete slabs dropped on him. The stallholder shrugged and said that he was a thief who had stolen a bicycle and who deserved to die. As the crowd grew to surround the body, we left the scene, really shaken by this episode, a reminder of how far we had moved from our previously sheltered existence and also a brutal introduction to a society where life was often cheap.

The Muslim school project led to an entertaining and fanciful proposal, which brought me again to the unrealized designs back home. There was talk of a possible new mosque to serve a growing Muslim population and this was to be funded by the Ismaili community, specifically their leader, the Aga Khan. For a practice committed to modernist design, it was considered to be an anathema to revert to a traditionalist model for any new solution. Before I left Ireland, I had been involved in the design of a new Catholic church in a rocky part of Connemara in the west of Ireland. We produced a model of a white reinforced concrete arched structure sweeping up from the chaos of rocks in a wild landscape. When this was presented to the Church authorities, they promptly rejected it: the design had moved too far from the traditions of Romanesque or Gothic, as the proper models for religious architecture. For the Kampala project, I produced a model in balsa wood of a simple elliptical vault in a thin concrete shell. In lieu of a glass wall, the vault was closed at each end with a lacy open grille to allow a breezeway through the building. In the essential reference to tradition, I included twin minarets, formed as slim concrete needles, but adding a dome seemed impossible. Predictably, the proposal suffered the same fate as the Catholic Church proposition: a polite but equally firm repudiation.

There was an official opening to the new school, which the practice had designed, and we were all invited to the ceremony. This was a momentous occasion for the community since the successor in waiting to the Aga Khan, the head of the Ismailis and one of the richest men in the world, was to be the guest of honour. We lined up to be presented to the distinguished visitor who arrived in a state car with the Governor of Uganda. A military and police guard greeted this handsome young man, dressed in a dazzling white suit. He strode around chatting to everybody. Mrs. Caffrey struck a predictably sour note later, when comment was made on the smart and handsome young 'prince'. 'I suppose he was handsome', she said, 'in a gippo sort of way.'

Building work was almost entirely carried out by Sikhs. Sites were a maze of thin pole scaffolding, lashed together with ropes and with long rickety ramps leading from the ground up to each level of the new work. In the early stage of building, these ramps had long lines of labourers running up and down, each with a wide shallow metal dish filled with liquid concrete which they poured into formwork for the emerging structure. There were often hundreds of workers on a project – a swarm of bodies and a babble of sound – but the structures rose quickly. This could cause problems for the architect who was inspecting the building to ensure that the work was being carried out properly.

The senior partner suggested one morning that I should accompany Alan and himself on a trip to the south and the town of Masaka where one of our new developments was progressing. He said he had reports that things were not satisfactory on the site and he wanted the visit to be unannounced. He warned me that there could be trouble. After hours of battling the atrocious roads, we arrived at the suspect site. A commercial building with shops on the ground floor and apartments overhead, the structure had reached the first-floor level with the concrete framework beginning to reach upwards. It looked perfectly normal and the Indian contractor, who was at first surprised to see us, began a sales pitch on the excellence of his work. Alec, in his usual way, stayed silent as we walked around and then asked us to return to the car and fetch hammers and chisels from the boot. 'This will be fun', said Alan, as we returned with the tools. Alec told each of us to take a hammer and insert the chisel about one inch above the bottom of each beam and to strike it hard.

After just a few tentative taps whole sections of the concrete under the first beam came away suddenly, crashing to the ground and just missing our feet. What was revealed was that many steel reinforcing bars were missing and the whole beam had been disguised by a neat plastering to mimic a properly reinforced concrete bond. The Indian boss was at first angry but then relapsed into a sullen silence as we set about his work, enthusiastically hacking lumps off his piers and hammering holes in the rest of the beams. When we stopped, Alec told the contractor that the whole structure had to be demolished to foundation level and that he would return in a week's time to check that the work had been carried out. At that, we walked slowly back to the car, I, at least, hoping that no large piece of concrete would be dropped on us from above. In the car on our return, the usually taciturn Alec told us that the building would certainly have collapsed if it had gone much higher. People could have been killed and the practice would have been held responsible. It was a valuable lesson. In a later report on the incident to the building's client, Alec stated that, 'much of the structure could be demolished with a one pound hammer.'

I was soon to have my own experience of drastic action. As part of my working day, I had to make inspections of other projects in progress. One of these was a large four-storey office building in the centre of Kampala. When I walked on to the site, I saw workers shovelling all sorts of rubbish, including clay from the ground, into a concrete mixer and this was being delivered to the floors overhead. I told them to stop and, after a walk through the site, went back to my car and drove around the block. I parked and went back into the site by another entrance, discovering that the same operation was going on with even more frenzy. Calling another halt, I went into the contractor's office and phoned one of the partners, who immediately ordered the work to stop, all workers to leave and the gates to be padlocked.

For some time our firm had been awaiting the arrival of an experienced clerk of works from Britain whose sole job would be to patrol and oversee each project. Jack Metcalf appeared soon after and proved to be a gift, leaving the architectural staff more time to design and produce the drawings.

Despite these experiences, most of the Sikh contractors were excellent, eager to embrace new ideas and co-operative in meeting the architect's often strange and difficult demands. The traditional architecture of Uganda in pre-colonial times was rooted in nature: the slender poles of the podocarpus forest; the thickets of bamboo: the long grasses of the savannah and the fronds of the dense papyrus swamps. These materials, allied to the unwavering red earth, created a truly organic architecture. The last manifestations of this tradition were in the great royal compounds of Buganda, Bunyora and Toro. Sadly, all that remained were little huts of the common people and these were often only in remote areas.

In the scramble to grab colonies in Africa, the European powers brought their own versions of architecture, which was often arbitrary and insensitive to an unspoiled and veritable

Garden of Eden. For the East African colonies, the arrival, over a comparatively short period of time, of huge numbers of Indians, first as indentured labourers and then as merchants and shopkeepers, brought a particularly utilitarian and frequently downright ugly expression of this exploitation of the land. Streets of towns were lined with mean blocks of concrete and plastered-over rough clay tiles, to provide shops on the ground floor and housing overhead. These very soon became streaked and stained with the red earth and there was no variety in the brutal monotony, which invaded every human settlement. Traditional architecture, on the other hand, had evolved with the changed circumstances and availability of new materials. The papyrus thatch, vulnerable to fire, gave way to a metal covering made by hammering used kerosene tins into flat sheets. The earlier high profile was retained, so the rusty roofs, married to the red earthen walls, were a softer if ramshackle intrusion into the landscape. Large hand-painted signs advertising 'The Happy Bar' and 'Sam's Pub' were typically cheery statements of individuality and enterprise.

The challenge for us, discriminating and trained architects from Old Europe, or so we thought ourselves, was to produce a Modernist style in tropical Africa. Le Corbusier had demonstrated, initially in Algiers, and then in Brazil and lately in the Punjab, how modern architecture could respond beautifully and appropriately to a hot and sunny climate. Another influence was the older and slower developing colonial architecture of the more ancient settlements of India and the Far East: the vernacular of the deep-shaded veranda, the slatted screens and grilles and, above all, the manipulation of breezeways to give natural ventilation throughout a building.

THE HAPPY BAR

The first priority of the architect was to see how design alone could achieve this goal of a livable building in a hot climate. Artificial cooling, such as air-conditioning belonged to the richer parts of the world; economics alone ruled out any such extravagance. The sun was king on the Equator. In the morning in this high country, the air was balmy after a night when the earth cooled, but by midday the sun shone vertically overhead and the cerulean blue of the early sky turned to a blinding white and an unbearable glare. The afternoon sun was the killer: west-facing façades took the full power of solar heat and radiated this back into the building, turning it into an oven. Le Corbusier had reinvented *brise-solei*, slatted sunscreens long used in eastern and Islamic architecture. His version of these was formed in concrete and could give an altogether richer and even mysterious feel to an otherwise dull rectangular block. Vertical slats could be turned at an angle to shade the western façades from direct sunlight, but a more interesting texture, giving a strong contrast of light and dark, could be achieved by the use of grilles in the traditional Islamic manner. We had most of these made on site, precast in lightly reinforced concrete, the contractors quickly and enthusiastically responding to the challenge.

This new world of creative activity was unbounded joy to me in those early months. There was a seemingly endless flood of new commissions: fresh schemes on the drawing board followed in quick succession, and out in the city and suburbs I could visit a growing number of my own designs now being built. It was a heady feeling walking on to a site and seeing the ideas on paper becoming real. There was also, undeniably, a sense of power when overseeing the work and knowing that it was your decisions that would shape the finished building. The dark side was that the responsibility for something going wrong was also yours, but youthful optimism usually managed to bury such thoughts.

Sometimes things did go wrong. A new bank on Salisbury Road was designed without windows for the large banking hall. Newly imported roof lights made in the form of plastic domes provided daylight. Unfortunately, in the first weeks after the celebratory opening, there was a torrential rainstorm, with tons of water thundering down on the flat roof. Leaks from the domes turned into a fine mist inside the high hall and, although this looked spectacular, it did not wet even a sheet of paper. The hot climate managed to evaporate the droplets as they fell. The owners, however, were not impressed, although it was they who decided that, for security reasons, no windows were to be provided. A solution was quickly found and the domes were resealed. We heard later that the rainstorm on that day was close to a world record, with eleven inches falling in a few hours.

An Indian corporation owned a huge sugar plantation outside the city. It was already one of the firm's biggest clients and keeping its owners sweet was important for the finances of the practice. British expatriates, many of whom were the sons of aristocratic families in the homeland, migrated from the colony of Kenya and once owned some of these big plantations. During the days of the notorious Happy Valley set in the fertile Rift Valley region of the White Highlands, the excesses of alcohol, drugs and extra-marital high jinks sent many of these settlers into bankruptcy. Entrepreneurial Indians were quick to step in and turn disasters into profit.

The commission was for a compound to house workers, and the clients were adamant that a high degree of security was required. To this end they directed that a high fence, with a gatehouse to control the entrance, should surround the compound. It was never clear whether this was to keep the workers in or to keep unwanted visitors out. We suspected that the former was more likely. After I had completed the drawings for this proposal, I thought that it uncannily resembled a Nazi concentration camp. The gatehouse was close to being a guardhouse and in an idle moment I produced a perspective sketch of the scheme, adding a watchtower with a cantilevered gun platform on the opposite side of the gate.

All that was missing was the chilling message *Arbeit macht Frie*. The partners were not amused and I was told to lose the sketch before the clients arrived to see the designs.

A more wholesome commission was from our first African clients, who had formed a co-operative to manage a large coffee plantation in the south of the country, close to the border with Tanganyika. As part of the expansion of this enterprise, they planned a training and visitor centre, with accommodation for prospective new farmers who wished to move from uneconomic smallholdings to seek bigger markets. The majority of our commissions came either from government or from wealthy Indian businessmen. The colonial government funded Makerere University and in one of the projects here I had the opportunity to use the thin concrete shell that had been jettisoned on the Islamic mosque proposal. The Faculty of Education needed a proper auditorium, so our proposal was for a wide elliptical vault of reinforced concrete: slatted concrete openings, without glass, at each end allowed for a breezeway through the hall. The auditorium was built remarkably quickly. The shallow rise of the vault allowed for easy access for the crowds of labourers to race up and pour the tons of concrete on the stretched steel mesh. Each night the roof had to be covered with grass to prevent the concrete from drying out too fast, and this gave the building a strangely bizarre appearance.

Kampala had a few cinemas, but none equated to the ostentatious 'dream palaces' which had mushroomed in Western Europe from the 1930s. The commission to design a new cinema in the city landed on my desk and became one of my most enjoyable projects. The client was an Indian entrepreneur,

AUDITORIUM, MAKERERE

an ebullient character and a huge enthusiast for Indian cinema. The design was to include shops and offices, but the cinema was to be the most advanced and luxurious in Uganda. Segregation by colour or race, while hardly ever overt in the country, was nevertheless imposed by sleight of hand. There was an entrance foyer and, at a higher level, a first-class foyer. When built, the lower level stalls had an overwhelmingly black audience, while the upper levels, where the seats were more expensive, were patronized by the whites, most of the Indians and a small sprinkling of black Ugandans.

When the complex was completed, the owner was beside himself with joy and promptly announced a competition for a name for his new project. Our offerings were mostly the hackneyed ones we knew: The Ritz; Roxy; Odeon; Savoy; Regent, but he eventually chose one from suggestions by the public, which he thought most illustrative of his beloved enterprise. It was to be The Delite. We were to arrange for the name to be erected in large letters on the front of the cinema. He said to me beamingly, 'Now I will be able to say at the opening, I am delighted to be able to welcome you all to the Delite.'

The inaugural film was 'Mother India', a renowned production from the growing Bollywood industry. It was almost a template for the flood of new stories from the Indian studios. Every narrative had the same theme and every story either a happy ending or a bitter-sweet one: poor peasant – downtrodden woman – neglected child – thwarted lover – betrayed wife, son, daughter: each of these exploited by a cruel employer, corrupt politician, estranged parent, dastardly philanderer but, finally, good triumphs over evil. The brochure for the official opening gave a précis of 'Mother India' that summed up the storyline:

> *Mother India is a story of a great, eternal proud woman – a portrait of a peasant woman, who could only be found in India. This is the story of her children – Ramoo and Birju. This is the story of Sukhi Lala, the village Zamindar, who thrives on the ignorance of illiterate peasants and lives on the blood of the poor. How Radha bravely faces and fights all odds and to protect the chastity of her culture and herself is dramatically presented on the screen.*

The heroines were invariably beautiful, slim and sinuous, and dressed in flowing silks of ravishing colours and glittering jewellery. The heroes were handsome devils, either smoking a cigarette with nonchalant ease or a manly curving pipe, while Clark Gable-style thin mustachios were a big hit. The glossy long black hair and elegant hands of beauties like the star Sheila Ramani featured on the film posters. There was usually at least one film from the west each week and these we welcomed because the predictability of the Indian scenarios could pall. 'The Drum', however, was just a Hollywood version of a Bollywood concoction. There was the stiff upper lip memsahib of the Raj, the British drummer boy and the malevolent Raymond Massey playing the evil Khan betraying the King. The sonorous tones of Paul Robeson in 'Sanders of the River' made a big impression on the mixed audience, even though the story was a travesty of African realities. Nuala and I both hugely enjoyed the performances of the great Charles Laughton and Robert Donat in 'Private Life of Henry VIII', but the drive back from the cinema in the black African night seemed far removed from the pageantry and pomp of Tudor England.

The owner of the Delite threw a big party after the opening and this was one of many Indian social gatherings we had attended. We were now experienced enough to approach the meal with caution, even though the host had assured us that the curry was very mild, especially cooked for Europeans. Invariably we almost burned our mouths. The drinks table was lavish as usual and it appeared that Asians seemed to think that all the British and Irish drink whisky, which was proffered in tumblers and would be rapidly refilled if you drank more than an inch. Staying upright at those parties could be a problem, but after some early episodes we learned politely to decline excessive hospitality.

Another dimension to this conviviality was the offering of gifts: we were assured that this was part of Indian culture. Christmas-time saw an avalanche of presents pouring in from contractors: usually bottles of liquor and baskets of luxury confectionery. The partners managed to appropriate most, but a few were handed out to the staff after the seniors had taken their pick. A darker side to this generosity was the suspicion of bribes. There was only one non-Asian builder, an Italian noted for his careful work. He confided to me one day that he had had to endure a lot of obstruction from officials in obtaining permits because bribes were often expected. When a builders' provider, who had submitted a tender to supply one of our nearly completed office buildings, heard that I was contemplating a weekend trip away from the city, he promptly offered me the loan of a large car and a new Rolliflex camera. I thanked him but declined, saying that a friend was providing a car and that I already had a good camera. I did not mention that it was a Brownie Box model. I had yet to afford anything like the Rolliflex.

We had not explored very far beyond the city, and the green hills and forests that stretched for miles through almost the whole province of Buganda. We were eager to see more of the country and particularly to travel west towards the vast game parks and the great mountains. After several months of intense work, the opportunity came to take a long weekend break. Walter, who had become a close friend to Nuala and me and whose boyish enthusiasm for all things new was a constant source of good-natured teasing, had just acquired a car. It was a second-hand Citroën, a low-slung machine that was sturdily built and seemed to be the appropriate vehicle for our first long-distance safari. This colourful term, borrowed from the white settlers of Kenya, came to be used for all trips of any great distance from your home. The Queen Elizabeth National Park had been newly established out in the western provinces of Ankole and Toro and along the borders of the Belgian

Congo. This was to be our first adventurous expedition to what we hoped would be a different Africa from the claustrophobic one of dense jungle we had experienced so far.

We set out early to try to cover the whole distance in one day, despite the primitive roads. After less than an hour we left the tarmac surface, ending with a sickening jolt as we passed on to the crude red murram track that led first due south before turning west. We reached the line of the Equator not long after leaving the last of the settlements. A large hollow circular monument in white concrete marked the divide, with 'North-South' painted on the plinth. Crossing the line for each of us was a first, so photos had to be taken. When we first hit the rough road, we thought that we would never make it all the way, despite advice given to us by old hands of up-country travel. The passage of vehicles turned the surface into a series of corrugations, and the trick seemed to be that a certain speed had to be reached and maintained so that the hammering of the corrugations was ironed out: too slow and you were shaken to bits, too fast and the same thing happened, except that now you could lose control and crash. It took some time to get the knack, although maintaining the speed when huge potholes appeared was impossible. Nuala was in a fairly advanced stage of pregnancy and the concern was that the incessant jolting might bring on the birth. She was determined to go on, however, and gradually we realized that the Citroën could handle the battering. Most of the time our vehicle sent up a cloud of dust, which seemed to stretch behind us for miles, but occasionally we ran into a rain shower that turned the surface into a skating rink of red slurry.

At Mbarara we turned due west and for some time we left

behind Buganda's suffocating density of tangled trees and tall grasses. The country now opened up to a vast savannah of short grasses and undulating low hills dotted with single trees and clumps of bushes. We saw our first wildlife along the road: small herds of menacing-looking buffalo which turned their heavy horned brows towards the sound of the car. To our delight, a herd of zebra raced away to the cover of a thicket. In quick succession we saw several types of antelope: the beautiful golden-hued eland, the waterbuck and the Uganda kob. Once we had to brake suddenly when a line of large ugly-looking warthogs crossed in front of us.

The landscape changed as we climbed into higher hills. There were fewer settlements here, which was a relief because every time we stopped for an essential toilet break, even when it seemed we were in the middle of a wilderness, at least one or two figures would materialize from nowhere to gaze silently at these white-skinned interlopers.

When we crawled and bumped to the highest point of the pass, a new vista of wooded valleys and ravines opened up, the road now snaking down to a level place where suddenly we were at the edge of an escarpment and the whole rift valley was below. We stopped the car and stared out at a wide grassy plain pinpointed with scrubby trees and could see, but still far off, herds of animals, some certainly elephants, the prime trophy of the Uganda game parks. Away to the west a dark mass of mountains marked the start of the Ruwenzori and, as I looked hard, I tried to persuade myself that above the heavy, brooding clouds that capped the heights, a flicker of white might be the fabled snows. This was the point where the Irish explorer Surgeon Major T.H. Parke became the first European to see the high snow-capped peaks. I wanted to believe that I too was one of the privileged to be granted this rare sighting. Nuala and Walter looked but concluded that the flash was just a high white cloud. I reluctantly agreed, but was more determined than ever to get to climb in that mythical wilderness.

After a long descent to the flat, we headed out to the Kazinga Channel and were now passing herd after herd of animals: wildebeest in dense, steaming throngs and more of the darkly frightening buffalo, an animal reputed to be aggressive and much to be avoided. Masses of antelope were leaping and dancing across the wide expanse of yellow grass, but the elephants were the real joy. We stopped time and again to watch the stately progress of family groups – huge matriarchs down to tiny babies – scuttling along under the legs of the mothers. We reached the Government Rest Camp just before dark, exhausted and grimy after our epic drive, but elated with this first African safari.

These camps were primarily set up to facilitate the officials, District Commissioners and others of the colonial administration, on their tours throughout the remote regions of the country. They provided very basic shelter, mainly consisting of large sleeping tents, each with a bamboo and grass outer roof for coolness in the heat of the day. A more substantial building usually housed a mess hall and kitchen. We loved the nearly primitive conditions and from our bunks, with only the mosquito net separating us from the dark outside, the sounds of the African night were exciting as well as sometimes hairraising. Below the camp on the water's edge we had earlier seen

AFRICAN SAVANNAH

large numbers of hippos. Their strange coughing ululations meshed with the sharp screams and howls of monkeys and baboons that crowded the trees around us.

Dawn was beautiful but brief. The first red glow in the dark eastern sky turned orange and the sun seemed to climb so quickly that we had to look away as the yellow ball turned fiery. The savannah came awake with the new day and all around us was an explosion of life.

We drove along a dusty track towards the channel, a waterway joining the smaller Lake George to the much larger Lake

Edward, names redolent of the Empire and the arrogance of the Victorian explorers who had 'discovered' this land. The hippos had retreated to the coolness of the water and the huge brown mounds looked lifeless until loud snorts scattered the white egrets standing sentinel on the backs of the animals. Masses of birds crowded the banks of the Channel – storks, herons and dozens of pelicans – but it certainly was out-of-bounds for us when we saw the primordial and scaly shapes of crocodiles half in and half out of the water.

Elephants were everywhere. We heard back at the camp that there were estimated to be at least 10,000 head in that one region. When we saw one group tearing branches off a clump of trees, we wondered how long it would take for the woods to be demolished. The animals ignored us as we drove slowly along, but we each had a tingling anxiety when we saw the huge, flapping ears and curving tusks turning our way.

On our way back the next day, we stopped for one last look over the plain. A small hillock a little way from the road promised a better view, so we walked out past tall cactus and the exotic euphorbia trees that were like giant inverted candelabras. The view was immense: the horizon of the table-flat land to the south dissolved in a violet haze, while to the west the foothills of the Ruwenzori were now a friendly bright green in the morning light. The summits, however, were still blotted out by that perpetual cloud. We turned to go and then heard a lion roar. It was far away but the sound was chilling as we retreated to the safety of the car.

CHAPTER 4

JACKETY MOJA – DOUBLE BRESTO!

The central market in Kampala was a spectacle, a tableau, and for us the heart of Africa.

WE WENT THERE EVERY SATURDAY, ostensibly to buy fruit and vegetables but also to enjoy the play-acting and vibrancy of an event that was an essential part of Ugandan life. After we had purchased our goods, with just a little haggling being the accepted norm, we often drifted over to the outdoor clothes auction. An Asian stood on a platform and held up each garment for inspection, calling out in Swahili, which sometimes sounded more like the Kitchen dialect of the language. This was a derogatory term used by purists for the original Ki Swahili of the coast and Zanzibar. The 'one jacket – double-breasted' brought catcalls and ribald laughter and most of the auction was noted for the great belly laughs of Africans who loved to joke and heckle, mainly in a good-natured way.

Uganda may have been a poor country, at least by European standards, but there always seemed, on the surface at least, to be a tranquil and easy-going ambience. Many of the walkers on the tracks near our house would play little home-made mouth harps, and the sound of popular African songs from wind-up gramophones spilled out from the shacks and roadside workshops all day long. The fertility of the land around the great lake may have been a major factor in the relative contentment of the people: everything seemed to grow here and there were no hungry periods in a country without seasons. The sliced-off tops of the pineapples we bought in the market, for instance, could be stuck in the ground in our garden and would promptly start to grow again. These luscious fruits were a specialty of Buganda, along with the huge bunches of little sweet bananas we bought every week. The equally prolific cassava, from which a type of flour is pulped, could always supplement the main food source – the green variety of banana, *matoke*, which grew everywhere. We never tired of the juicy pawpaws, growing all year in our little garden, although our houseboys, we thought, were secretly amused that we loved these, to them, pedestrian fruits.

In those early months in our newly adopted country it was easy for us to embrace the colour, gaiety and endless daily sunshine as a veritable paradise garden. Any dark sides seemed just small interventions: we could shrug them off as isolated incidents, not troubling our nearly idyllic lives.

Nuala's job as a secretary in the Department of Education meant that our two salaries were now helping to reduce the loans from the practice and we felt we could indulge our hunger for music with a good record player. Long-playing records were newly available in East Africa and a leisurely browse in the capital's one music shop on a Sunday morning became a weekly event. In our early enthusiasm we bought a new long-playing record each week: Don Giovanni's declamatory arias may have sounded alien in the African night, but they gladdened our hearts out in the bush. Dylan Thomas's rich intonation of his own *Under Milk Wood* was played again and again until we almost had this lyrical and funny work off by heart. A cold beer on the terrace of the City Bar, where we could meet friends and watch the Sunday promenade, rounded off the morning ritual.

Most Sunday afternoons we would drive to Entebbe. Out there on the open shores of the vast lake, the breeze would be cool and we could sit on the grass under a shady tree. Many of the government officers lived here and their bougainvillea-draped bungalows with deep verandas were on rising ground facing out over Lake Victoria. There were no shantytowns like the notorious Katwe, whose chaotic tangle of ramshackle settlements and teeming population we passed on the main road from the capital. The sweeping, well-kept lawns, the impeccable Botanic Gardens and avenues of beautiful trees gave more of an impression of an ideal old England, with sunshine of course, or indeed of a transplanted Simla from the days of the Indian Raj.

At first the sparkling water and little sandy shore tempted us to go swimming: the hippos, we were told, were few and emerged only at night when they would trample holes in the manicured lawns. The crocodiles, we were assured, kept well out towards the little islands. It was, nevertheless, usually a quick dip and a wary look-out. A much more frightening revelation came with the warning that bilharziasis had been discovered in the lake water. We read, to our horror, about this disgusting and potentially fatal condition. A parasitic fluke, apparently, sought out a host snail to develop larvae, which later emerged in the water and could penetrate the

ENTEBBE, LAKE VICTORIA

skin. They then wiggled their way into your bloodstream to feed. Our swimming instantly stopped. The most worrying aspect was that the diagnosis might surface only after a long period, maybe a year or more. It took a while for the worry about consequences from our earlier bathing to fade, although in time we would become blasé about the litany of direful portents presented by the old Africa hands. Snakes and deadly insects usually featured in apocalyptic yarns, following the stock dangerous animal stories.

I did, however, have one unpleasant reminder of what Africa could inflict. One day, after a walk wearing open sandals over a stretch of short grassland to a rocky hillock, I noticed a small black bruise under one of my toenails. I wasn't particularly bothered until a week or so later when I discovered that the bruise had grown considerably and was in fact an insect that had burrowed under the nail and was now feeding happily on my blood.

Lake Victoria offered other diversions. Walter's next enthusiasm after the purchase of the rakish Citroën was to buy a boat. Entebbe had a small sailing club, and the model favoured was a 17-foot wooden craft that evidently made up a special class – the Lake Victoria Sharpie. The club was almost exclusively white. There may have been the token Asian or African, but they were not evident and the club, with its rules and clubhouse bar and lounge, would not have been out of place in Britain or Ireland. Walter asked me to crew for him while he practised handling the boat. Our sailing usually took the form of a slow cruise out into the lake, enjoying the hiss of the water and the cool breeze away from the land. Inevitably Walter was persuaded to enter one of the weekly races. He had become a member after the archaic custom of having his name put up for election: 'I could be blackballed by the toffs in the club,' he said jokingly.

I did crew for him, along with a messmate from the Bachelors' Quarters who had just arrived from Nairobi. This individual was called Parker; we never knew whether this was his first or his last name, but we did know that he was a Kenyan with the attitudes to race commonly held by settlers from the White Highlands. He was a large, heavy man and, even though Walter and I were both skinny and light, the boat dipped perceptibly when we got in. After one of our usual clumsy starts, we trailed after the grandiloquently named 'fleet'. We were a long way last as the others vanished to round one of the small islands beyond the peninsula. The earlier gentle breeze was growing stronger as we prepared for our turn around the island when, out of nowhere, a sudden squall of gale force tore across the lake and in seconds the boat overturned. I was caught inside the upended hull but managed to pull myself down and over the side to the surface. Walter was already holding on to the hull, but Parker was floundering and in a state of panic. He chose that moment to yell that he could not swim. We pushed him up onto the upturned boat where he lay spreadeagled and hanging on to the centre-board. This had the effect, however, of sinking the hull lower in the water and Walter and I were now almost immersed. We knew that it was possible to right the craft, although neither of us had any experience of this operation and the fact that an over sixteen-stone body was weighing down the centre made our task seem insuperable.

No other boat was in sight and we quickly realized that the island hid us from view of the shore. We were about a hundred yards from this oblong, low-lying, but thickly wooded piece of land, which had a fringe of dense reeds hiding the banks. We did not mention it, but looking at that hidden shore the dreaded thought had to be voiced – croco-diles. Parker got even more panicked but Walter reminded him that he was practically out of the water while we were up to our necks in it. We tried to remember what we had been told to do if we ever found ourselves in this situation. Was it to kick and make a lot of noise or was it the opposite and to stay absolutely still? I think we tried both until we realized that our actions were probably counteracting each other. The boat was now drifting slowly and we hoped it might edge towards the point of the island where we could be seen, but very soon it was obvious that we were heading towards the reeds and whatever might be skulking there.

'Where the hell is the rescue boat?' said Walter after what seemed like hours but was probably less than twenty minutes. The wind had almost died away in the lee of the island and we had now settled into the routine of alternatively kicking vigorously and staying completely still. The rescue boat had come tearing around the point, but we hardly noticed it until it was practically on top of us. Parker was plucked off the top of the hull and dumped on board while Walter and I were helped over the side. An officiously expert yachtsman jumped into the water and tugged the boat into the upright position, its sodden sails still intact. Walter and I got back on board and started the task of bailing it out. Parker was kept on the rescue craft that escorted us back to shore and, although nothing was said to us, we felt chastened.

The sudden change in the weather that day was a rude shock after our early months in Uganda when we experienced a seemingly endless succession of days of blue skies and hot sun. Lake Victoria was usually the engine of weather change and during the two short rainy seasons it seemed we could predict when rain was to be expected. Mountainous blue-black clouds boiling in from the vast inland sea often obliterated a fine morning by early afternoon. Spectacular forked lightning stabbed down from the clouds and by the time the rolling thunder meshed with the lightning, the rain came in a cataclysmic inundation. We drove home to our house on Mbuya one late afternoon in such a deluge. Our track had roaring red torrents tearing new channels in the surface and, when we made it to the house, there was an opaque waterfall from the roof over the veranda through which we dashed. In storms like this, everybody got soaked, but few minded because inevitably the sun came back and the whole earth began to steam.

The sailing club and certainly the Top Club were exclusively white and most sports tended to form groups based on race. A newly arrived young Englishman moved into Walter's quarters and announced that he wanted to play football. He had played for a well-known club in Britain and was considered to be a star player. The Top Club heard about him and immediately asked him to join their team. The lad, however, had done his homework about Uganda soccer and announced that he would be playing for the top Kampala team, all African. His fellow whites were outraged at his crossover, but his reply was that he had no interest in playing useless football. We went with Walter to see him play in one of his first games and it was a joy. Africans played with great élan and the crowds were ecstatically noisy but with huge joviality. The new star darted down the field time and again in sweeping side-steps that delighted the crowd who roared 'Bwana, Bwana, Bwana' each time he took the ball. The Bwana or Sir was the respectful way to be addressed by servants, so the roar had a sarcastic tinge to it, but it was, without doubt, a good-humoured one as the crowd were plainly enraptured that the 'star' had chosen to play for their team. The derogatory term for white men was *muzungu*, but this was never used to your face in those days.

Nuala and I had an early introduction into African society when the firm's young Mugandan draughtsman, Pius Kiyuima, announced his forthcoming marriage and invited all the office staff to the ceremony. We gladly accepted and were given directions to the venue – a small village some way out in the countryside. On a glorious Saturday afternoon we set forth on the one-hour drive west of the capital. To our surprise, the seemingly endless forests that surrounded the city gave way quickly to more open country – short grass meadows dotted with single graceful acacia trees, some draped in frothy yellow blossoms. An occasional flame tree flaunted its shamelessly scarlet flowers: it was an splendid setting for a wedding.

Pius warmly welcomed us and introduced us to his family, but we were surprised that no one else from the practice had turned up: in fact we were the only white faces in a sea of happy smiling Africans. The ceremony was conducted in the little Catholic church: a simple rectangular building, white-washed and with a red-painted corrugated iron roof. Afterwards, in the brilliant sunshine, there was a group photographic session and, to our astonishment, we were placed in the centre of the picture, next to the bride and groom. Pius, in his dark suit and spotlessly white shirt, was beaming with delight beside his sparkling bride, splendid in a voluminous and dazzling white dress.

ACACIAS

A few days later in the office Pius handed me a letter that was addressed to Mr. and Mrs. Rothery:

I have much pleasure in announcing that this gift of a fowl has been chosen for you two by my wife from those we received from her parents in thanking you the benefit and kindness you shown us on the 28th of June.

A short story on marriages in Buganda as a custom of Baganda only.

After the wedding party, the parents of a girl ask their daughter to go and fetch food which she will cook for her husband.

Among these presents you will find such as these:
Bananas, matoke, goats, fowls, ground nuts, onions, mush-
rooms etc.
So in the same way we have already come to the same thing
as such.

Wishing you a happy and a long life
I remember here yours faithfully

Pius Kiyuima

We were touched at the thought of the gift but a little taken
aback that the fowl was still alive, legs trussed and handed
over in the office squawking furiously and with feathers
flying. Like Queen Victoria, Mrs. Caffrey was not amused.
With difficulty we got the chicken into the car and back to
the house where houseboy Peter delightedly accepted it. He
took it away, promptly wrung its neck, plucked it and we had
it for dinner that night.

My Sikh colleagues in the office shared little of their lives with
us. The older man did not appear to have much of a life
outside work, while the younger, Mohinder Singh Chana,
gave a definite impression that he had, but no details of this
leaked into office gossip. He did, however, let one interest slip
out in a conversation during a morning break. He was an
enthusiast for speedway racing, but as a spectator and
definitely not as a participant – he was too much of a dandy
for that. On his recommendation, we went along one
weekend to see the sport at a ramshackle stadium in the lower
part of the city. The racers were all Sikhs and the daredevil

manner in which they tore around on their motorbikes brought howls of appreciation from the mixed, largely Asian and African, crowd. Spectacular crashes were frequent and these usually had the rider lose helmet and turban, with the resultant fall of luxuriant jet-black hair and catcalls from the spectators.

Apart from the Sikhs and a smaller number of Goans, who were mainly Catholic, by far the largest population of Asians was Hindu. They owned and ran most of the businesses and even small shops in the capital and indeed in all the larger towns. Their dedication to work was absolute but during the great Hindu festival of Diwali they would break out in exuberant celebration. This was a festival of the New Year: according to the Indian calendar, it took place in October and was celebrated by fireworks and lights in honour of the goddess of good fortune. The fireworks were supposed to banish the spirits of the dead, but in Kampala it seemed to be mostly an excuse for unruly elements to throw firecrackers at passersby. During Diwali, streets were best avoided after dark.

A much more joyful, animated and often hilarious after-dark frolic erupted with the coming of the flying grasshoppers or ants. In some seasons countless millions of these would invade the city and almost blanket each street lighting standard. Crowds of mainly young Africans would gather masses of insects, eat some on the spot or carry them home to fry as an exceptional delicacy. We were told that they were delicious and crunched like nuts, but we could not bear to try.

Relaxation for the white expatriates was more sedate and

predictable. Nostalgia for 'home' dominated. The dinner party became an established ritual, usually involving a round of reciprocal entertaining of colleagues, at least in the early days before more genuine friendships were formed. These obligatory evenings could be a strain: a common subject of conversation was the servants, their idiosyncrasies and unreliability, but just occasionally an understanding as well as appreciation of a parallel view of the world. We had Jack Metcalf, our clerk of works, to dinner one night. Jack, a middle-aged Cockney, had a spate of stories, and after an evening of jokes and laughter our houseboy, who had been beaming all the time he served the meal, announced, 'He was a wonderful man, was he not?'

'Yes, he was very funny', we said.

'Oh no, it was his white hair', said Peter. This manifest respect for the *mzee*, the Swahili term for an older person, turned our perceived hierarchy of youth and age upside down.

A later houseboy, John, had long conversations with Nuala about the difficulties he was having in obtaining a wife. His prospective bride's father was demanding an exorbitant price in cattle before giving his consent, and John was worried that he might never be able to afford marriage.

Our friend Jean was an attractive young woman and after she and her husband had left one night, John remarked, 'How much did her husband have to pay for her? Do you know?'

Nuala replied, 'Nothing.'

'You mean she was free?'

'Yes.'

John went round the house later, muttering, 'Free, free.'

The approach to our house on Mbuya hill was through a

short stretch of dark forest after we had left the city's limits and the last street lamps. We had been warned of the danger of cars being stopped on this section at night and were advised to carry a weapon as protection. Guns were not allowed, although across the border in Kenya many of the white population were armed. I began to keep a short length of iron bar on the floor of the car and handy to my right hand if I was attacked. If our guest for the evening was an unaccompanied woman, then we escorted her back to the city after dark, following in our own car.

One night I was trailing an Irish doctor friend, Carmel Gibson, into the first lighted section of the Jinja Road when I saw her car come to a sudden halt. I jumped out to see what was happening, to discover a body lying at the side of the roadway and Carmel bending over to examine it. Another car was stationary and skewed across the side channel while a terrified Asian man was babbling away to Carmel. It appeared that he had hit an African pedestrian who, although prone on the ground, seemed conscious. The driver's immediate concern was the sudden gathering of a small crowd and an imminent hostile reaction. He was in genuine fear for his life and with good reason. Carmel, however, had sufficient authority as a doctor to take control, at least for a short while. As the crowd grew, she asked for help to place the injured man in her car and I quietly told the Indian driver to slip into mine. We drove off quickly. I dropped the driver, still shivering with fear, at the nearest police station, while Carmel took the injured man to the main Mulago hospital where he was treated and found not to be seriously hurt.

These sporadic dark episodes could easily be buried when,

day after day, the sun shone from that high African sky and each night the stars blazed in the inky black. Nostalgia for home, however, was never far away for even the longest and most settled expats. Inevitably, talk of 'home leave' would drift into the debate at those dinner parties. Government employees were entitled to four months' paid holiday every three years and since this included the whole family, it was greedily valued. My parsimonious contract never looked more unattractive than when the talk was of three-week cruises up the Red Sea and across the Mediterranean and splendid summers in the Lake District or west Cork or even the newly blossoming resorts of France and Spain. Home leave for us was still too far away to contemplate, but it was difficult not to feel envy when animated holiday stories were being shared.

We hungrily anticipated letters from home. The general post office was only a short walk from our workplaces and it was tempting to stroll at lunchtime up the avenue of jacaranda trees on Grant Street to check our post box. Most of the time it was empty, but now and then the familiar blue airmail letter appeared, usually with news from family. When the opened box revealed a fat white envelope, we knew that this was from one of our friends back home and would have a wealth of gossip that would have us wallowing in nostalgia for days.

The course of our lives changed for ever just before our first Christmas in Uganda. Nuala gave birth to our son Eoin in the European Hospital in Kampala a few days before the festival. After one particular visit to her and the new baby, I arrived back at the house to be told by John that he was off for his Christmas holiday: the implication was that I would have to look after myself. Whatever about Nuala's increasing cookery skills, I had none: having both a wife and a houseboy did not encourage me to achieve any. My festive celebrations that year consisted mainly of cornflakes and a bottle of whisky!

Our household ménage now increased with our servant quota rising to three. All the old Africa hands said that it was essential that we have an *ayah* to take care of the baby: it was just not done not to have a full complement of servants, we were told, even if Nuala decided to give up her job to stay at home. She had hardly arrived back with our baby son when the first hopeful *ayah* aspirant was waiting outside. We had no idea, in our recent status as employers and as new parents, how to make the right choice. Mary was a chubby Mugandan with a wide smile. She presented a tattered and faded piece of paper which appeared to be a reference describing her in that stock phrase as 'reliable and willing'. We hired her on the spot – our inexperience was almost certainly greater than hers. Nuala stayed at home for the next few weeks and our lives settled back into a new routine. John, the houseboy, kept a polite but distant space between himself and the *ayah*. He even adopted a small air of dignity which was close to disdain. No baby's nappies were allowed in his wash basket and Mary would have to circle around his kitchen domain when she did her work. With the two of them trying to avoid each other in the house, we would retire to the veranda and pretend that we were really the bosses. The honorific 'Memsahib' and 'Bwana' were still not sitting easily on our shoulders.

Mary's time with us did not last very long. One day she announced that her husband had to depart for another town and a new job. She left us on good terms and we did not have to wait long for a replacement to turn up. Erinora was a lanky and somewhat laidback individual who went about her work in a gaudy dress and with a high degree of non-involvement. It was quite common for the *ayahs* to take their charges, slung expertly on their backs, out on a walk to the local shops. However, we learned that Erinora was ranging more widely with Eoin. The suspicion gradually dawned that she may have been a part-time 'working girl' in one of the shacks on the main road. We knew that Africans loved and cared for children, so had little worry that any harm would come to him, but it was clear that Erinora had to go.

Our next *ayah* turned out to be a treasure. No sooner had Erinora departed than Sarah arrived and announced herself to be qualified for the job. She was a Kikuyu from near Kisumu in western Kenya – a tiny young woman with a solemn expression. She took charge at once, could manage Eoin expertly and was not intimidated by houseboy John. Her husband, Benjamin, had been taken on as servant in one of the other houses in our small group, so a measure of security seemed possible. Our lives began to run more smoothly and Nuala was soon able to resume her job in the city.

One evening after Eoin was well settled and the houseboy and *ayah* had left us alone, we heard distant shouting from the lower part of the hill. Noises at night were not uncommon. There was a scattering of huts in clearings in the forest below us where Africans often called greetings and carried on long-distance conversations in the stillness of the night. This sounded different, however. Now there was a sense of violence in the agitated voices. Less than an hour later we heard someone running up to the veranda and banging on the outer screen. It was Sarah. She was crying and hardly able to speak. Eventually, in a mixture of Swahili and English, she told us that Benjamin had been taken away by the police and could we do anything to help? I asked her if she knew where he had been taken and she said yes and could guide me there. In the car, more of the story unfolded. It appeared that the Gombolola or Saza, the provincial police, had taken him and that it was merely a matter of the non-payment of a local tax. Sarah, however, suspected another motive – prejudice against her husband's Kikuyu tribe. She was afraid for his safety because the police who had arrested him had first beaten him up.

We drove down to the Port Bell Road and then turned up a narrow track in pitch blackness: the headlamps lighting up thick liana-draped forest trees on hairpin bends until we came out on the top of a hill. There was a crude, unlit, block-work building on the summit, but in the car lights I could see a large iron-barred doorway. I left Sarah in the car and walked up to the building. In the darkness I could just make out a number of figures standing silently inside. I called out for Benjamin, and eventually he was pushed forward to clutch the bars, but said nothing as an officious-looking individual, presumably a guard, came up to me and asked me what I wanted. This was the stage when a bit of white man author-ity might work, I thought, and I adopted a lofty tone and demanded to know why this man was being detained. Chanc-ing my arm, I said that he was my employee and I wanted him back. The surly guard was not cooperative, so I told him to fetch his supervisor. A more amiable character arrived and

I modified my demand to asking what action was required for Benjamin's release. A short period of verbal horse-trading led to an indication that if a certain sum were to be paid, he could be released. After handing over this relatively trivial amount, the barred door was unlocked and Benjamin set free. He and Sarah thanked me on the way back, but his employer, who was away at the time, never contacted me later. It could have been of course that Benjamin was too embarrassed to tell him his story.

The old Africa hands, while congratulating us on our new status as parents, were now renewing their cautionary tales of the hidden menaces of Africa. The biggest threat was snakes. Snake lore, after the iniquities of servants, of course, was a favourite conversation piece at dinner parties. Horror stories were told with gusto and if you believed half of them, you would never set foot out the door. So far the only snake we had seen was the odd one coiling across the road in front of the car. The experts loved to pontificate about the precautions that must be taken for any safaris on foot: the main one was to carry an antidote in case of a snake bite. The trouble appeared to be that different antidotes could be required for diverse species of reptile. The corollary of this was that you should have an expert with you on every outdoor walk to identify the beast that had bitten you. Sensible people told us that most snakes get out of your way fast, but you don't go reaching into dark holes or under rocks.

The day came, however, when we had our own snake story. We arrived back one afternoon from work to find the *ayah* standing on the veranda clutching the baby. John and most of the other houseboys were creating a hullabaloo and charging all around our garden shouting and beating the ground with sticks. I asked John what the fuss was about and he told me that there was a *nyoka*, a snake, and a very bad one at that. Everybody seemed to be enjoying the hunt but I wondered at the folly of bare arms and legs for the chase. The snake was eventually surrounded and enthusiastically beaten to death: the dead body was then triumphantly carried up and presented to us. Unlike the pencil-thin reptiles we had often seen coiling rapidly across the road, this one was huge: six feet long and as thick as a human arm. The grinning houseboys forced open its jaws to display the incredibly sharp teeth, which had the desired effect of severely unnerving us. I tentatively reached out to touch and was surprised that it did not feel cold and slimy, as I had expected. The coils, draped over my arms, were surprisingly heavy, while the almost iridescent dark green scales, merging into deep indigo, felt warm and sensual. It turned out to be a black mamba, one of the deadliest snakes in the world and when we asked our most mordant expert on Africa what to do if a mamba bit us, his reply was, 'You have less than twenty minutes. Start digging.'

The next domestic crisis we liked to call 'the long night of the ants' came not long after the snake incident. Occasionally, on one of our walks in the forest below the house, we would notice columns of ants scurrying along the forest floor, making a visible indented track in the earth and fallen leaves. We usually took care to step away from them, because, like ants anywhere, they would have a nasty bite. Out in the more open savannah the huge red pillars of anthills were a common feature of the landscape, but we never felt threatened by these industrious insects. One evening, just after dark, John came back to the house in an agitated state, calling us to come and see. Outside the gable end of the house was a huge column of red ants, millions of them, flowing along in an undulating torrent that seemed endless. On each side of the column were lines of larger soldier ants, whose pincer-like jaws were longer than their bodies. These faced out, ready to defend and attack anything that came near. John called them safari ants, which, presumably, were on their way to establish a new colony. The drive went on and on and a deeper and wider track was all the time being beaten into the earth with pebbles, small stones, leaves and twigs being pushed aside by the swarming bodies that seemed at times to crawl over each other. It was a fascinating but intimidating sight and a reminder of the power and indifference of the insect world to our human one.

Our mood as interested observers changed when we noticed that a breakaway smaller stream of ants was heading for our open rear door and starting to enter the house. Eoin was asleep inside in his cot and we rushed in to try to divert the new column. Brushing the insects aside did not deter them for long and we just got bitten. John had experienced such invasions before and came back with a tin of kerosene. We carefully poured this in a line all around the house and set it alight. The diverted stream soon rejoined the main flow and we stamped out the remaining invaders inside. The safari went on for hours. After it petered out, there was an extraordinarily perfect channel in the ground to mark the passage of the multitude.

Rumours of an increase of burglaries, as well as our new

responsibilities as parents, brought the Cassandras out in force.

'You have to get a dog,' we were told.

The animal had to be a proper guard dog, not any little cuddly toy. This was largely the advice of the various experts, and Parker, Walter's messmate, vehemently argued the case for a guard dog. He said that he could find us the ideal type and a few days later he and Walter turned up with this large animal perched on the rear seat of the car. We looked dubiously at the tawny, heavy-jowled creature, which appeared less like a potential pet than something that belonged in a cage.

'He is a Rhodesian Ridgeback and his name is Socks,' Parker said.

The four white paws and endearing name slightly softened our reticence and we agreed to take him in. We had never heard of this breed before, but in the weeks that followed we learned some unsavoury facts about the Rhodesian Ridgeback. Evidently it was trained, or actually bred, to develop an antipathy to black Africans in the racist and white-dominated societies of Southern Rhodesia and South Africa. As Eoin began to play outside, under his *ayah's* eye, little children of the various servants from other houses often joined him. We were getting quite unsettled about the animal, which had few appealing traits and neither John nor Sarah could be relied on to control it when we were out. A crux was reached with the gift from a friend of a tiny Siamese kitten for Eoin. We had had it only a couple of weeks when, one afternoon, Socks attacked it and tore it to pieces.

I grabbed the brute, pushed it into the car, and drove into Kampala. At the Bachelors' Quarters I delivered it back to

Parker, telling the story of the kitten and our fears about the African children. He wasn't in the least put out, thinking it was all a big joke. Walter agreed to take care of the dog and told us that he would be confined within the compound. We were relieved to be rid of the animal, but Parker's attitude rankled. Walter invited Nuala and me to dinner in his place one evening and at some stage Parker joined us. He told us stories about his time in Kenya and the Mau Mau uprising.

Governor Sir Evelyn Baring had declared a State of Emergency in the Colony of Kenya in October 1952. He had arrived in Nairobi only a month earlier, in response to the growing violence in the territory. The genesis of the Mau Mau, however, can be traced back to the arrival of the first British settlers in 1902. Over the next fifty years the fertile highlands of the colony were effectively taken over by white farmers. The lands were seized from their original owners, the Kikuyu people, who were increasingly either forced out of their traditional grounds or hemmed in by the vast estates of the newcomers from Britain. The colonial authorities failed to respond to the increasing discontent over the land appropriations. Militants' soon ousted moderates in the African nationalist groups, particularly the Kenya African Union, led by Jomo Kenyatta. The Mau Mau initially terrorized their own Kikuyu people into supporting their violent rebellion, but the declaration of the Emergency, and the arrival of the first British troops in October 1952, turned the campaign into a widespread conflict. When the colonial government allowed local militia to be organized, the violence became nasty and bitter. The most notorious of these militia was the Kenya Police Reserve.

Parker then let drop the fact that he had been a member of the KPR. This group was recruited mainly from the white settlers in the colony and for some time their brutal behaviour was being increasingly exposed and condemned. They had engaged in savage reprisals for Mau Mau atrocities, as well as the widespread repression of the general Kikuyu population. He openly boasted of his time in this discredited force and arrogantly argued the superiority of white rule in the colonies and that Kenya would never and should never get independence.

That same year, 1957, the Gold Coast became Ghana – the first African state to cede from the British Empire. *Uhuru*, 'Freedom', was now clearly emerging on the horizon for Uganda.

KUNGU

CHAPTER 5

KUNGU TO MUHAVURA

A few miles outside Kampala a great tooth of naked rock poked up from the forest floor.

THIS STRANGE FEATURE was called Kungu. It seemed to be such an aberration in the lush greenery that it was inevitable that the local population would accord it some kind of mystical status. To me, however, and to my newly acquired friends in the Mountain Club of Uganda, it was a gift from heaven – a perfect playground for rock climbing. The frantic pace of those first few months in Africa – home settlement, combined with the intensity of my work – pushed the desire to climb far back in my consciousness, but soon the passion to challenge high places reasserted itself.

Where could I start? The obvious first step was to find others with similar desires and not least some local knowledge and skills. To my surprise, I discovered that a Mountain Club of Uganda existed and appeared to have an membership of almost two hundred! Alan Warner of Makerere University was my first contact and later became my main climbing partner. The membership figure for the climbing club turned out to be more aspirational than representing a realistic number of regular climbers. There was, however, a small hard core of dedicated individuals who carried out most of the work, such as hut-building, and who had explored and climbed in most of the wild mountain ranges of Uganda. Like Alan, several of these were teaching in Makerere, while Biddy Lynam, a geologist, based in Entebbe, was an enthusiastic builder of huts. She was a sister of Joss, the founder of the Irish Mountaineering Club. Except for a handful of names in the list, most members were European: the few others were mainly Asian, with one notable exception. Tim Bazarrabusa, a Ugandan from Fort Portal in the west of the country, was an important figure in the foundation of Uganda mountaineering and was later elected president of the Club. The Uganda Mountain Club had a number of African schools and colleges as affiliates and there was certainly no colour bar. This was a notable departure from the more subtle 'whites only' policy practised by other clubs formed by expatriates,

I soon found out that the majority of the individuals named on the club list were there for social reasons, rather than for having any zeal for mountain-climbing or much less rock-climbing, my particular passion. Many of the Europeans in East Africa worked for the government and this meant that large numbers were away on home leave, at least four months, at any one time, thus further reducing the pool of possible climbing partners. My initial excitement at the prospect of finding a vibrant climbing community similar to the one we had left in Ireland soon diminished. Nuala had often partnered me on climbs but the challenge of vertical rock had not the same passion for her and, in any case, in those early months in Africa, she was pregnant.

It did not take long, however, before I managed to make contact with a small number of like-minded eccentrics who relished the problem-solving gymnastics of finding different ways of reaching the top of this improbable pinnacle in the forest. Kungu now became the main venue for Saturday afternoon climbing trips. My first visit was with Alan late one afternoon, with only about two hours before darkness. A tiny track led from the road head through tall elephant grass and past a few *shambas* of banana plants carved from the thick forest. Suddenly Kungu was there – a somewhat menacing presence rearing up from a small clearing. No wonder it could be seen as a home of spirits. For me, however, this was just the sort of challenge I had long been denied since those days of glorious effort on the crags of Wicklow and Donegal. Who cared about spirits? I was more worried about snakes. Although the rock was only just over a hundred feet high, it was truly vertical, but a great crack in the middle split the massive rock in half and offered a fairly easy route to the flat summit. Alan and I sat there looking out over the huge forest which stretched, it seemed, for ever, but with the African sunset dropping fast, we managed to rope off the top before total darkness. Starlight flickered through the tree canopy as we blundered back through the forest in the black night.

It was inevitable that curious onlookers would be attracted to watch our climbing antics. These seemed to evoke amusement rather than offering any offence to the 'gods' of the rock. When Brian Kavanagh, an Irish head teacher from Namilyango College, near Kampala, brought groups of his older students on climbing trips, it appeared to satisfy the locals that it wasn't only the *mzungus* who were mad. This did not prevent an enterprising individual from announcing himself as a guardian of the spirits of Kungu and setting himself up on Saturday afternoons to collect a fee to satisfy the 'gods'.

It was an escaped murderer who brought the end of sport-climbing at Kungu. Matiya Kigaanira was convicted of murder in 1955 after a bizarre incident that resulted in the death of an African policeman. Kigaanira had established himself as 'The Prophet of the Tree', preaching about Doomsday in the treetops while various efforts were made to get him down. Blandishments having failed, he continued to taunt the police and in the end one constable climbed up to persuade him to come down, but tragically he fell to his death. The 'Prophet' denied that it was he who pushed him and shouted that a plague of rats had swarmed out of the forest, attacked the policeman and eaten him. The story was not believed, however, and sentence of death was passed, this being later commuted to twenty years' imprisonment. After a few years Kigaanira escaped from prison and made his way to Kungu where he again established himself on high and proclaimed that the gods had lifted him from jail and transported him to the top of the rock. Here he pranced around, waving a spear and hurling stones down on anyone who tried to get close. He had brought plenty of food and was enjoying his fresh elevation as a prophet.

The authorities ignored him for a while, but Ugandans love any kind of unusual event and the Kungu Prophet soon attracted a circus, with hundreds travelling from Kampala to see the fun. First the Fire Service tried to hose him off the top, but the flow of water was not strong enough or the ladders high enough to reach him. The crowd had now grown to over a thousand and police feared that there might be a riot. The area was quickly cordoned off and the Mountain Club was asked for some climbers to help the police get close to him. Kigaanira shouted down that he would ask the gods to close the great central crack, the only easy way up, and that anyone trying to climb would be crushed to death. Furthermore, he said that huge snakes, each with heads the size of a man, were guarding him. Only two climbers responded. Most were reluctant to get involved in what could turn out to be a disaster, but this pair, with the help of the police distracting the target from below, overwhelmed Kigaanira and lowered him to the ground. With Independence Day fast approaching, the incident did not help relations with the soon-to-be outgoing government. This growing hostility gave hero status to the 'Prophet of the Rock' and the Mountain Club advised that visits to Kungu should cease.

A spider's web of roads surrounded Kampala. The main spines of this web led out into the hinterland and until the early nineteen fifties these main roads were little better than tracks – narrow, rutted, rolling and coiling up and down every hill and hollow. A new road-building programme, initiated in 1954, concentrated on these essential spines, widening and straightening them and, most importantly, ironing out the endless hills and hillocks, albeit by brutally bulldozing right through the softly green landforms. The new roads, however, did mean that it was now possible to explore more remote areas of the country in a shorter time.

One of these new highways went directly north towards Lake Kyoto and a place called Nakasongola. There were rocks here to be investigated and a quick expedition was planned one evening in Alan's book-lined house on the Makerere campus. Alan and I set off just after dawn on a clear Sunday morning in his Morris, and outside the city the new road pointed straight north. Although the line was now carved through the low hillocks and filled in over the innumerable depressions, the surface was still unsprayed red murram and was already racked into endless corrugations. Since we were now becoming expert at dealing with these, the car was pushed to its limits, trailing great clouds of dust. After about two hours, the forest and green bush gradually opened out into a wide savannah, dotted with single trees in the short grass. The road turned into a narrow track until the landmark we had been told about, a solitary tall mvule tree, appeared in front. We left the car and walked towards a long dense thicket until a curve in the path revealed a wide gap and there the two enormous rocks called Wajala and Nansambya were revealed.

I had grown tired of the dense forest and green bush that surrounded Kampala and felt suffocated by the sense of enclosure there. It was intoxicating to stand now under the hugely expanding sky of intense blue that spread wide over the plain of yellow grass. The two great rocks were smooth and rounded, each like an enormous stranded whale. We sat on a fallen log to gaze silently and let the tension of the long, hot and rattling drive ebb away.

It was soon time to get down to business: there were new routes to be made on these lovely rounded volcanic outcrops. There would be time enough for relaxed meditation when we reached the top.

Wajala offered an obvious way up: a shallow groove

meandered past a scrubby bush with a small ledge for resting
about one-third of the way up. When we were established
here, there was a wide view out over the plain and suddenly
a voice called out from far away. Alan, who was a fine linguist,
called back. What followed was a typical Lugandan conversation, consisting of a long stately succession of greetings and
responses. The caller, now coming closer and closer, wanted,
after all the formalities were completed, to know what we
were up to. He finally appeared at the base of the rock and,
without pause, scrambled up to us. He was wearing a long
tattered white *kanzu* with bare feet. He told us his name was
Kassim. The ascent of the groove continued while our new
friend climbed alongside us, his toes splayed wide to seek
footholds. It felt ludicrous to continue our orthodox climbing routine – one person belaying while the other led upwards
with the safety rope firmly attached – while all the while
Kassim, unroped, continued his own parallel line, chatting
away cheerfully. After he finally left us, continuing a long
drawn out farewell, I ruefully decided that I could not fairly
claim the first ascent of the climb with the privilege of choos-
ing a name. It just had to be called Kassim's Groove.

Several more new routes on both rocks were crafted and
this time it felt justifiable to name them for future aspirants.
Towards evening Alan produced the bottles of beer that had
travelled inside a canvas water sack attached to the front of the
car – the standard African method of keeping water cool on
safari. We felt deserving of this treat, sitting there watching
the sun's descent over the western horizon. It was a long drive
back in the dark, but we were content.

Our first year in Africa was nearly ending and I was getting restless. My two goals for our move to Uganda were architecture and mountains. In those early months I had seen more of my designs realized than in my whole six years since graduation, but no big mountain had been climbed. It was time to plan. The Ruwenzori had to be the top prize, but preparation for this would take time. All the high mountains of Uganda lay along the edges of the country. The Ruwenzori bordered the Belgian Congo to the west, and all along the frontier from Sudan to the north and Kenya to the east were continuous ranges of high hills, culminating with Mount Elgon at 14, 178 feet. To the south, however, and bordering the junction of the frontiers of the Congo and Rwanda were a group of eight high volcanoes. Bufumbira and Virunga were alternative designations for this fascinating area; the former was favoured in Uganda, while the latter was commonly used in the Congo. A party from the Mountain Club was planning a trip there and we eagerly joined up.

I had fallen in love with the names of these hills: Vishoke; Karisimbi; Mikeno; Nyiragongo; Nyamlagira; Sabinio; Mgahinga and Muhavura. They sang of Africa: their superb cones, seen in photos, were sometimes tipped with snow. I had first read about the volcanoes in a rather strange book entitled *Alone to Everest*. The author, Earl Denham, is pictured on the frontispiece wearing a voluminous but immaculate white anorak, the hood firmly fastened around his neck. He is leaning on a long ice axe and with his neat Clark Gable moustache stares out with a faraway dreamy look. As a training exercise for his solo attempt on Everest, he planned to climb in the Ruwenzori, but for some reason, not fully explained in his book, this trip was abandoned and he turned to the Virunga volcanoes, eventually climbing all eight.

The first half of Denham's book deals with his adventures in Africa over several months in 1946. He paints an intriguing picture of battles with bureaucracy, the most difficult being the Belgian colonial authorities in the Congo where five of the volcanoes were located, but the enduring theme throughout is that of the lone white man amongst the 'natives'. Livingstone, Speke and Burton were his heroes, he says, and certainly his doomed attempt on Everest, one year after the Virunga adventure, was in the tradition of those early explorers. His definition of 'Alone' in his title, however, seemed to ignore that fact that with him he had Tenzing and Ang Dowa, two of the most experienced Himalayan Sherpas. Six years later Tenzing, with Ed Hillary, reached the summit of Everest.

Although Walter had no great interest in mountaineering, he was excited about a trip down to the highlands in the extreme south-west of Uganda and asked to join our group. We were delighted since we dreaded the prospect of our little Fiat trying to struggle up the steep hills of the provinces of Kabale and Kisoro, and negotiating the atrocious roads from Kampala. Walter's Citroën was certainly up to the job, but he insisted on borrowing a model with a bigger engine for the trip. This Citroën was built like a tank. One bad feature, however, was that the gear lever was on the dashboard and brute force was often needed to shift gears. Nuala and I were to travel with Walter and share the driving, while baby Eoin reclined in his wicker basket on the rear seat.

The group set off early in three cars: after the tarmac was left behind, we each tried to avoid the other's dust clouds but early rain dampened down the surface and the cars could stay closer and give one another help if any faltered. This turned out to be an epic journey because the short rainy season was upon us. Shortly after Mbarara and turning southwards, we came down a steep hill to find the hollow at the bottom deep in water. The first car that tried to cross got stuck in the middle and immediately a crowd of Africans ran out from where they had been waiting at the side of the road for just such an event. They heaved and pushed, singing and laughing, along with the passengers, who had to get out into knee-deep muddy water, until the car was back on the other side of the flood. This was done to cheers from a further crowd watching the drama. The exercise was repeated for each of the other cars and when they were all assembled on the far side, it was time to thank our saviours and, of course, pay a little for the service. The whole exercise was conducted in great good humour and it was undoubtedly more for fun than profit. The same stoppages were repeated at least three more times before the long climb began to the highlands of Kabale. The final barrier was not water but a huge sea of creamy mud. Again we found a willing army of helpers, but we were all caked in red until a roadside stream allowed us to wash our legs and feet.

We stopped near a small village just before the start of the steep switchback climb to the high pass of Kanaba. This was to cool off the engines, refill radiators and generally have a rest. Nuala lifted Eoin out of his basket and, with me carrying him, we walked up to the village. We no sooner came in sight than a horde of villagers raced out to see these strangers.

LAKE BUNYONI

We were surrounded in seconds by an excited mob but it was soon apparent that Eoin was the focus of attention and not Nuala or me. One person explained that they had never seen a white baby and so he had to be put on display. Some were fascinated by his hands and wanted to see if they were white also on his palms. They were reluctant to see us leave and followed us back to the cars, waving goodbye.

The serious climbing began after the town of Kabala and all of us were tired and relieved when the 8,000 feet Kanaba Gap was surmounted. The country at the first of the lovely lakes, Lake Bunyoni, was truly beautiful. It was a scene from the English Lake District; wooded islets and waving grasses at the shoreline and only the occasional little group of round, papyrus-roofed huts made you sure it was Africa. It was cool up there also – almost chilly – and we were told there were no crocodiles or hippos in these waters. Was it the cold water or because of the lava deposits all around? Nobody seemed certain, but this was healthy country and we reveled in it after the hot and often humid world some four thousand feet lower beside Lake Victoria.

It was dark on our arrival at the Travellers' Rest Camp at Kisoro. This was sited near a British customs post and just short of the frontier to the Belgian Congo. The enterprise was the work of Mr. Baumgartel, a remarkable man who had dedicated himself to the study and protection of the mountain gorilla, a species unique to the country of the great volcanoes and a shy and rarely seen animal. Baumgartel was eager to tell us about his great enthusiasm but we were all far too tired and suggested a session with him after our climb. A quick meal and we were glad to slip into the comfortable bunks. Eoin was already asleep and we followed him soon in the stillness of the African night.

After an early breakfast, the party gathered on the veranda to stare out at our first view of the volcanoes. The gentle lakelands were behind us but spread wide in front was a panorama of stupendous drama – this was the very centre of Africa, where the molten core of the earth had gushed out millions of years ago and solidified into these massive but elegant cones. Close to where we stood, the huge bulk of Muhavura reared up and the early rising sun sharpened the edges of the deep gullies – black clefts that ran down from the summit to be swallowed by the forest. Its much smaller

SABINIO

neighbour, Mgahinga, was connected near the forest upper edge by a saddle, but its summit was already developing an early cloud. The star performer of this morning drama was Sabinio. It stood splendidly alone, a perfect cone in a vast flat sea of deep green which seemed to flow to infinity. Away to the west loomed the other volcanoes, the farthest lost in a shimmering haze. It was easy to imagine hearing the music of Africa, the haunting, repetitious, rising and falling cadences floating over the land.

Sabinio was the one most coveted, but negotiations with the local Gombolola Chief for a guide on the intricate tracks to the mountain informed us that he would need at least two or three days to arrange for paths to be cut through the thick bamboo forest that ringed the lower slopes. We just did not have the time to wait, so we settled for Muhavura, which was closer and needed far less path-cutting. It was also a feasible one-day climb, albeit a very long day. The booking of the services of a guide had already been arranged. His name was Reuben and Mountain Club members knew him to be knowledgeable and reliable. The Chief then blandly informed us that another party had already set off with Reuben. We felt aggrieved that he had been pinched from us, but the Chief said that he had another man who was an expert on the routes up Muhavura. This individual turned up shortly and announced his credentials. His name was Tomasi and his dishevelled appearance was not very encouraging. He wore a long ragged overcoat with buttons missing, tied around his waist with wisps of grasses. His pockets were bulging with, presumably, his food supplies and he carried a panga, a long knife with a broad blade that was usually razor sharp and served as a tool as well as a weapon. He tucked this under his arm as he shook hands.

While Nuala stayed back at the Rest House with Eoin, the rest of the party set off for the base of the climb. At this stage, ominously, clouds had boiled up from the minor peak and covered the main mountain right down to the forest. The necessity for a local guide to the lower part of the mountain now became apparent. There was a substantial scattered population in little settlements all around the lower slopes and this resulted in a maze of little tracks criss-crossing each other through the scrubby bush. Our guide strode on, seemingly confidently, and we began to have more faith in him. Every now and then we passed some locals, and others would call out to us from hidden huts. Conversations would start sometimes before other travellers were met and then continue without stopping until the voices faded away.

As the slope steepened and the first bamboo forests appeared, Tomasi became less certain and our steps were retraced several times until, frustratingly, the track appeared to go in a complete circle right back to where we had been twenty minutes before. At this stage the slope had steepened so much that I surmised that the final slope of the mountain had begun. I suspected that our so-called guide had never climbed far up the mountain and decided to override his advice and take the party more or less straight up. There had not been much need for Tomasi to use his panga to cut a track and, except for an odd swipe at a trailing thorn or a clump of stinging nettles, he carried it more as a token of his status as a guide. We had hoped in the early zone of the densely green forest to have at least a glimpse of a gorilla, but it was not to be. The noise and disturbance created by a party of eight clumsily crashing along this overgrown trail were enough to scare off all wildlife. At this stage the bamboo was not too dense and the little tracks were now in a general upward direction. An occasional break in the forest gave magnificent views back down to the bright waters of Lake Mutanda and the rolling green hills sparkling in the sunshine, which was now eluding us on the increasingly darkened mountain.

We passed the final edge of the forest and the way up was now fairly clear, although the mist was swirling around us. At one stage Tomasi insisted on crossing over one of the deep gullies and up to the other side. Reluctantly we agreed to this change of direction, since there was a definite track winding down and up to the other side. Losing height is always a test of morale, but after we struggled down 200 feet and then back up to the far ridge, the route now seemed to point straight up. The slope was unrelenting, without any change of gradient or flat platform for resting. Most of the party was now tiring rapidly but when the mists were briefly torn away by a rising wind, we saw tiny figures of the earlier group far up the slope. This view seemed to charge our team to fresh energy and we caught up with some of the first party stretched out exhausted on the heather slopes. They told us that the top was only 500 feet up, but this I did not believe from long experience of the innumerable 'false summits' that frequently fool climbers.

The zone of fantastic high altitude vegetation peculiar to East African mountain regions was now in sight. This weird semi-forest appeared out of the gloom of cloud quite suddenly – giant lobelia, groundsel, celery, parsley and other European plants, magnified to grotesque proportions. The masses of fallen and dead stalks were soggy and slippery and progress was difficult. The effect of altitude was now beginning to tell and some of our party were feeling queasy. We had, after all, come in two days from 4,000 feet at Kampala to now nearly 13,000 and had not properly acclimatized.

A heather bluff dotted with tall lobelia appeared out of the mist and there was the summit, a tiny plateau of short grass around a perfect little crater filled with water. There was no view and the cloud was dark. It was bitterly cold at 13,547 feet. Most of the others straggled up to the top at intervals and there was soon a circle of pale sickly faces sitting down for a cold lunch. When a late member of the party reached the top, he reported that one person had stopped about 500 feet below, unable to continue. He was in a safe place and had decided to wait for us to descend. It was imperative not to

MUHAVURA

miss him as we went down since there was no discernible track in the tangle of dead vegetation. When the retreat from the summit began, we called out to him and, after a slightly worrying few minutes, a distant hail pointed us through the thick mist and we found him sitting miserably and shaking with cold. He was suffering from, of all things, an ingrown toenail that had nearly crippled him. Helping him to his feet, we took turns to support him to stumble down the slope. Almost everybody was feeling the effects of altitude and most had to pause at intervals to be sick. I joined the affected and threw up several times. The fact that I had just consumed a tin of herrings, washed down with an orange drink, may also have been a factor.

Tomasi was also behaving strangely, lurching about as if punch drunk or maybe it was the local brew he had brought with him. At one stage when he was chewing on a large loaf of bread with one hand and holding his panga with the other, he stumbled, tripped on his straggling coat-tails and fell headlong. He appeared to have fallen on his panga and we could only watch with horror as he slid down the slope. His descent was halted when he came up against a tall lobelia and we were relieved when he got to his feet and continued his descent, still nibbling on his loaf, which he not dropped and still holding the panga, which was not blood-stained.

A storm broke as our party reached the edge of the forest. We were soaked to the skin in a few minutes. It was late now and gloomy as our slow descent continued in an eerie green light. We began to think of the possibility of sitting it out in the darkness and the prospect of leopards and gorillas prowling around us. The struggle through the dense lower slopes continued until the daylight went and we now had to cross ravines that had become roaring torrents of water blackened with lava. After more than two hours of us stumbling through the dark, the road head and the cars finally appeared. The lights of the rest camp welcomed us at the end of the bumpy track. It had been twelve hours since our start on that bright morning.

Despite our tiredness, we stayed up late that night, being regaled with tales about Baumgartel's beloved gorillas. The lowland gorillas of West Africa had been well known and studied from the middle of the nineteenth century, but the existence of the completely separate species of mountain gorilla had been discovered only in the early years of the twentieth century. All the stories of these animals attacking humans were nonsense, according to Baumgartel. They were quite timid and the roaring and chest-thumping of the big males, he said, was only to scare off possible threats to his family. The Belgian colonial authorities across the frontier in the Congo had a strict policy of protection and care of the gorilla population. Such an enlightened attitude to the wildlife seemed at variance with its discredited approach to the peoples of this enormous European possession in the heart of Africa. Baumgartel was battling for the same protection to be extended into the volcano region of Uganda, particularly because of the inexorable extension of settlements up into the animals' forest domains. His parting words to us as we eventually dragged ourselves off to bed were 'there are too few gorillas in the world and too many humans'.

The next morning, as we stood for a last look at the magnificent vista, Tomasi appeared on the veranda. After a prolonged and decorous exchange of greetings and pleasantries, the delicate matter of his guiding fee was slipped into the conversation. This was accepted in a dignified manner and, as he departed, he paused on the steps and, looking up at the mountain we had just climbed and that now shone clear and brilliant in sunshine, solemnly announced: 'That is Muhavura, all the way from the bottom to the top.'

CHAPTER 6

THE MOUNTAINS OF THE MOON

The car plunged into a cloud of white butterflies just outside
Mityana on the road to the west.

THERE WERE HUNDREDS of thousands of them: a
blizzard of fluttering bodies that covered the
windscreen and, against the bright sky, floated down
like huge snowflakes. We had never seen anything like it and,
when the car stopped, the tire-marks were black, as if traced
through a dusting of snow.

Ralph Naylor and I were on our way to the Ruwenzori. At
last, my dream of the big mountains was near reality. Months
of planning and searching for suitable companions had led
to Ralph, a science lecturer in Makerere University, agreeing
to join me. He had climbed a little with me on Kungu and,
although he had limited experience of high mountains, was a
steady and, I hoped, reliable companion for the adventure.
He was quiet and shy but I was confident that his calm
personality would be invaluable in the difficult conditions we
expected in that remote wilderness. We were to pick up a
third prospective member of our little expedition at Kasese,
where he was due to arrive on the train from Nairobi.

I had not managed to recruit any member from the

Uganda Mountain Club: the pool of available and suitable climbers in the country was just too small. Ralph and I decided to place an advertisement in one of the main East African newspapers announcing our expedition and inviting candidates with sufficient experience to join us in the enterprise.

It was my belief that we should look for a third climber to make up the party. It came from a conviction, after much reading of mountaineering literature in my younger days, that three was the safe minimum for travel in wild places. If a climber were to be hurt, then one could go for help while the other could stay with the injured person. Planning our strategy one evening, I joked with Ralph that the policy of having a minimum of three keepers on isolated lighthouses arose from the experience that when only two were employed, one could murder the other and then say that he had fallen into the sea. I had also read of that strange manifestation known as 'the third man on the mountain' where two climbers, isolated for long periods, felt the strange presence of a ghostly third following them in the mist.

We had only one reply to our advertisement. It came from a Kenyan expatriate named George Bentham, who claimed to be a fit and experienced alpinist and eager to climb in the Ruwenzori. We took him at his word and invited him to join us. The railway had been extended across Uganda to the town of Kasese with the main purpose of serving the mines of Kilembe, in the eastern foothills of the great mountains, and George decided to take this more relaxed route rather than face the long drive from Nairobi.

It was this railway that finally opened up the Ruwenzori

for serious exploration. Stanley had not accepted Parke's first sighting of the snow-covered peaks in 1888, but a month later he saw them himself. His comment, in his report, was to cement the view that he alone was the first to confirm the existence of the fabled Mountains of the Moon: 'My eyes were directed by a boy to a mountain, said to be covered in salt, and I saw a peculiar-shaped cloud of a most beautiful silver colour, which assumed the proportions of a vast mountain covered with snow.'

When the railway from Mombasa on the coast of the Indian Ocean reached the port of Kisumu on the eastern shore of Lake Victoria in 1901, the whole interior of East Africa had opened up. Gone was the necessity for huge caravans to march for months from the ocean, and many parties now tried to climb the highest peaks of the range. All these early expeditions, however, failed to reach the high summits. The enormous difficulties of access, combined with the often atrocious weather conditions, defeated the ascents of all but a few minor summits.

This all changed in 1906 when the splendidly named Prince Luigi Amadeo di Savoia, Duke of Abruzzi, arrived in Uganda with the best-organized and well-planned expedition ever to attempt a serious exploration. This mission was structured with almost military precision. There were over 300 porters, six scientists and four of the most experienced Italian Alpine guides from Courmayeur. The party included an outstanding photographer, Vittorio Sella, whose stunning views of the landscape of the Ruwenzori were published in the official account of the expedition in 1908. They climbed all the major peaks, naming them in the process, and, most importantly, produced the first definitive map of the range.

Surprisingly, it was twenty years before the next successful ascents were made, this time with a much smaller expedition, led by the early Everest climber Noel Humphries. W.H. Tilman and Eric Shipton, that indefatigable pair of adventurers, made the third ascents of the highest summits in 1932 and this effort was notable for its economy of scale. In two weeks the pair climbed the three main peaks, sleeping under rock shelters and pushing themselves through long days for a light-footed sojourn in this still pristine wilderness. Tilman wrote about their exploits in his 1937 book, *Snow on the Equator*, a title I have borrowed. I had met him at the Alpine Club in London a year before we went to Africa: his experiences inspired me and I now hoped to repeat his and Shipton's ascents of Mount Baker, Mount Stanley and Mount Speke.

It was fifty years after those first ascents by the great Italian expedition that I set off with Ralph in his Morris Oxford on a June morning for the 206-mile journey to Fort Portal. The car was crammed with equipment and supplies: tents, sleeping bags, ice axes, boots, crampons, ropes, cold weather gear, rucksacks, stoves and cooking utensils. Food had to be packed in separate bundles, waterproofed and ready for individual packs for the porters. A roof rack was omitted because of the bone-shattering roads, so everything had to be stuffed into the boot and on the rear seats. We wondered if the suspension would stand the load. We were exhausted when we reached Fort Portal, the only large town on the western rim of the country, but following a short rest we pushed on the last fifty miles to Kasese.

There was no room in the car for George, so Ralph

dropped me off at the turn for the mountain track to the village of Bugoye and went on to meet him at the railhead. I was in a near silent landscape when the car disappeared down the road. Standing there for some moments before the walk up to the village began, I became aware that there were no habitations nearby and the feeling of being totally alone was vaguely disturbing. There had been talk of lions in the area and in my solitary state the urge to look behind me every now and then was hard to resist. The village came in sight after about two hours and Ralph and our new companion appeared soon after I arrived. Up here the altitude was 5,000 feet and the air was cool and pleasant. An Asian house, attached to the Kilembe Mines Power Station, provided a camping site, because we were too tired to go on to the road head at Ibanda village, where our porters were waiting.

George was tall and gangly, and at first meeting seemed taciturn to the point of aloofness. He was quite vague about his occupation in Kenya, just remarking that he did 'this and that'. I surreptitiously checked his equipment, noting his new boots, ex-army rucksack and long wooden ice axe. This was little different to Ralph's and mine since army surplus was the mainstay of mountaineers in the early 1950s. However, instead of the unbalancing Commando rucksack with its punishing steel frame, I had acquired a proper climbing sack in Chamonix in 1953. George was even more non-committal about his mountaineering experience, but our enthusiasm to get on our way pushed aside any concerns about this. It was only a short drive to the road head and I managed to squeeze into the Morris, sitting on top of the folded tent.

The village of Ibanda, situated near the banks of the

Mubuku River, was the home of the Bakonjo people and the base for the porters and guides to the vast region of forest and mountains rising above. The Bakonjo, often referred to as Konjo, are a small ethnic group straddling the frontier of Uganda and the Congo. They are hard-working and self-reliant, as are most mountain folk. The climate up in the uplands was healthy, there was abundant clean pure water and crops grow well and as a result survival rates, by African standards, are high. Polygamy is accepted but since a high bride price is always demanded, sheer economics is often the main motivator for the monogamous state. They are known as a relaxed, open and a good-humored people, where a new joke would be passed around for weeks.

A large crowd of villagers, men and women, met us at the edge of this little settlement of red clay-daubed huts, each roofed with banana leaves. One individual stepped forward when we got out of the overloaded car and gravely introduced himself as Wambali and announced that he was to be our headman and guide for our expedition. Through the Mountain Club it had already been agreed with the village chief that a head guide would be chosen for us and that he would be responsible for recruiting the team of porters for the trip. We had brought all our own food supplies and equipment but we were also responsible for providing the food for the African porters. Here again the Mountain Club was highly efficient in negotiating an agreed daily ration as well as acceptable load weights. An Asian storeowner, Ahmed Bhimji, based in Fort Portal, was contracted to supply the provisions and to have everything transported to his small *duka* in Ibanda. The store provided us in advance with a printed list of the daily rations required for the porters, set out in exact and meticulous detail. It consisted of 2 lbs. cassava flour; 1 lb. groundnuts; 1 lb. smoked fish; 1 oz. sugar; 1 oz. salt; 1/8 oz. tea and 2 cigarettes. The cassava was grown by the Bakonjo and ground by the women into a flour. Although *matoke*, green bananas, was the preferred main diet for Uganda Africans, cassava flour was much more portable and seemed to be preferred by the local people. The smoked fish came from Lake George and according to Ahmed Bhimji's leaflet 'A week's notice is necessary for ordering fish.' To further facilitate prospective Ruwenzori adventurers, the store had all these supplies made up into 50 lb. loads.

In addition to the food, each porter had to be given one blanket, one sweater and a pair of cheap tennis shoes. The blanket and sweater, also supplied by Bhimji, were thin and cheap-looking but not a single porter carried his quota up into the mountains. Most wore ragged shirts and shorts, while tattered tweed jackets and old torn sweaters were also favoured. Bare feet were preferred, even when we reached the snow. We suspected that the new blankets, sweaters and shoes had been sold. Finally there was the question of payment: this had to be in cash and the required denomination was the Uganda shilling. These coins or *shillingi* were carefully counted out for us in a Kampala bank and then housed in a large stout leather bag. It seemed to weigh a ton.

The plan was to hire 14 porters in addition to the headman: eight of these to leave when we reached the head of the Bujuku valley, while the remaining six would be kept on for the walk out. A crowd far larger than the prospective team now surrounded Wambali and we kept well away from the

arguing and excited pleadings that were now providing enter-
tainment for the remaining villagers, mainly women and
children. It was several hours before the final team was
selected and the headman could allocate a load to each porter.
The Bakonjo were relatively short in stature, as many
mountain people are, and our team was a mixture of young
and old. There were a few grey heads, no doubt friends of
Wambali, but all were in high spirits, and smiles and laughter were the response as each load was pointed out. Everything was packed into sacks that were hauled up on to backs
and then held by broad bands around the forehead. Every
porter had thin spindly legs and, as each was loaded up, they
trotted around cracking jokes with the admiring spectators.
The unfortunate one who was allocated the paraffin tins and
primus stoves did not object even when the porters' metal
cooking dishes were clapped on top of his pack.

One man was given the heavy leather sack of coins to
carry and we had a moment of consternation when, with a
huge whoop of joy, he grabbed the sack and ran off up the
track. The others howled with laughter and we relaxed and
entered into the spirit of the game as the procession slowly
snaked off up the trail. It was, however, a moment of relief
when we caught up with the 'money man'.

It did not take long for our high spirits, at least those of
the *bwanas*, to subside: the well-worn track petered out as we
entered the long elephant grass where the undergrowth was
criss-crossed with thorns and nettles. In addition, clouds of
stinging insects nearly drove us to distraction. George was
now beginning to show worrying early signs of being less than
able to cope with difficult conditions. He seemed unhappy

and every bramble appeared to trip or tear him. Later I heard him swear at the porters: their continued high spirits were apparently annoying him. Wambali was in front wielding his panga to clear any trailing thorns and vegetation from the now overgrown and almost invisible track. The three of us stayed towards the rear of the group, as several of the porters, also armed with pangas, joined the headman to clear the path. After an hour or so the party halted and everybody went silent. There was an air of tension and eventually a whispered word was passed back along the column, '*tembo*'. It appeared that elephants were up ahead. We could hear nothing but it was a little unsettling that the Africans were obviously nervous. As we moved on, now more slowly, the tall grass thinned and we came out into a wide flattened strip, a veritable roadway smashed by a herd of elephants and leading more or less in the direction we were going. The sight of a huge pile of dung, still steaming, meant that the animals were not far ahead of us. There was a distinct feeling of apprehensiveness as we almost tiptoed along, dreading that the herd would come thundering back.

Up to now the trail had been almost flat, the walls of ten-foot high grasses around tall trees meant that we could not see where the first rising shoulders of hills would lead to our way upwards. Wambali suddenly stopped and pointed to a section of the wall of grass: three of the porters dropped their loads and, with the headman, attacked the vegetation with pangas and then disappeared into the forest. Ten minutes later they returned and the column followed the newly cleared path that led to where the elephant grass ended. There was now a definite rising line through a thinning forest and we could at last see the high dark hills around us. The tension fell away and the high spirits of the porters returned with jokes and catcalls. George's humour had not improved, however, and he was having trouble with the growing steepness of the slope. Now and then, when his swearing and groaning grew louder, we could see the porters smile and sometimes snigger. They probably already had a nickname for him and no doubt also for each of us.

The climbing eased on to a rocky promontory or spur, open to the sky and offering a tremendous view over the forest. There below, in a wide clearing, was a herd of elephants: the one we had just avoided. The porters gathered around laughing and pointing excitedly, saying how lucky we were not to meet them. They assured us that from now on there were no wild animals to threaten us, except leopards. These, we were told solemnly, were very dangerous. Ralph and I smiled, having being told similar stories many times, but George, a city man, looked fearful. We let him sweat.

The ridge now narrowed, with occasional dramatic views out through the beautiful podocarpus trees that dominated our progress. The porters were spread out well ahead of us but the way up was clear. At one point we caught up with one man who was fashioning a little shrine at the side of the trail. This consisted of a tiny rounded hollow of plaited grasses with morsels of nuts and beans, which, he said, was a gift to the Gods of the Mountain. The going was easier now through thinning trees and there at last was the Nyinabitaba Hut, at 8,500 feet. This was a basic timber shelter perched on the ridge but after a nine-hour hard trek could not have been more welcome. The porters clustered under a huge overhanging rock and soon had a cooking fire going. Our primus stove gave a warming glow in the rapidly growing darkness as we cooked our tinned meal but we were too exhausted to stay awake for long. The furniture of the hut consisted of two low canvas beds. We drew straws for these, because rats were a problem. I lost, and slept on the floor, alternatively covering my head in the sleeping bag to avoid the rats running over my face or uncovering it to prevent suffocation. Deep sleep took over and I soon forgot about the scuttling and scurrying noises all around me.

It was a bright morning, with the sun shining and the shapely Portal Peaks towering over our campsite. Where was the notoriously wet Ruwenzori weather we had been expecting? Everybody had recovered from the previous day's ordeal and on a lovely cool morning our high-spirited group strode off along the ridge. The Portals, with their steep rocky summits soaring clear of the dark forest fringe, were our first sight of the high peaks and a foretaste of the greater snows and glaciers to come. The bamboo forest was the next zone of vegetation to appear and progress through this was slow and frustrating. The route from the Nyinabitaba Hut led downhill for about 500 feet until we finally reached the banks of the Mubuku River. Although we had been following the line of the river all the way from Ibanda, this was the first time we had actually seen it. A roaring torrent of brown bog water faced us, while Wambali and the porters clustered around arguing about the best way to make the crossing. A previous party had stretched a log across to make a safety handrail but this had been washed away and now stood upright and firmly wedged downstream. By a desperate scramble upstream we found a flatter, wider and shallower section and the porters began wading across through freezing waters. The huge rounded boulders in the stream were slippery, but provided resting places to hold on to, yet everybody still got soaking wet.

The infamous high altitude bogs now appeared. The going was exhausting where pools of black liquid mud, separated by high grass tussocks, tested our resolve. Every step was an effort, as we alternatively tried to balance from one tussock to the next or sank knee-deep into the glutinous ooze. The giant heath forest now loomed ahead, a weird and silent world of fantastic tall heaths draped in hanging lichens. These outlandish manifestations of our mountain heathers were up to 50 feet high and their spindly branches and trunks were cocooned in blankets of moss and liverworts. At ground level the rocks and fallen stumps were covered by soft carpets of electric green mosses, moulded and rounded into shapely and sensuous forms. It was a magical scene as we worked our way up the Mobuku gorge to the great rock shelter of Kabamba. Huge overhangs thrust out from the mountain wall and under these the ground was almost dry, a relief after the bogs and dripping forests. The porters had a fire of dry heath stalks going in minutes and it was a real pleasure to stretch out in this high eyrie at 12,000 feet. That night the sky was clear for the first time since we had left the lowlands. I walked out in front of the overhang to gaze up at the stars: sparkling pin-points of light in the blackness. The Milky Way blazed a broad swathe across the heavens. I could clearly see Orion at one end but the Southern Cross seemed lost in the galaxy.

It was very cold at this height; the sheltering rock wall and roof did little to ease the chill from the hard ground. We awoke at dawn and tried to start the stoves while still wrapped in our sleeping bags. The porters were huddled in their blankets around the dead fire and would not stir until eventually one man revived the embers and soon had water boiling to encourage the others to move. It was not until 9 am, however, that we could finally resume the climb upwards to the Freshfield Pass and, if we were lucky, have the first view of Mount Stanley, our ultimate prize,

A cruelly steep slope brought us out on to a flat traverse and into a further zone of extraordinary vegetation. Gigantism was in full play here, with common garden plants magnified by high altitude to prodigious size. The most spectacular were the giant lobelias: mature specimens were like elegant obelisks towering to over 20 feet from a perfect fringe of green spikes. The giant groundsels or seneccios were only a little shorter but with bushy heads and masses of brown dead leaves on their stems. The beautiful helichcrysum, with its silvery grey foliage and pale yellow flowers, added to the prospect of a mythical garden in another world. Shrouded in mist, the tall plants looked like ghostly figures and it was impossible to judge scale and distance. A sudden gust of wind and the clouds were torn away and there before us were the shining snows and glaciers of Mount Baker, fine against a blue sky. Energized by this sight, we almost raced the last hundred feet or so to the top of the Freshfield Pass, hoping for that view of Mount Stanley, renowned by Vittorio Sella's magnificent photographic panorama of the peaks, but denied to so many Ruwenzori travellers.

Our joy was short-lived as the inevitable mountain

weather closed in over the peaks, but at least the top of the pass was clear and we could appreciate the amazing colours at this altitude of 14,200 feet. Deep yellow mosses predominated, interspersed by patches of russet, with young lobelias dotting the ground with their bright green sprouts. On our left the gaunt, grey, lichened walls of Mount Luigi de Savoia rose up into the mist, and on our right we saw the start of the ridge of Mount Baker, the planned route for our attempt on the peak.

It was downhill now to the Kitandara lake and our resting place for the approaching night. The slope steepened and we slithered and tripped repeatedly on the masses of sodden and rotten plants that covered the route. We tried to zigzag to avoid helpless slides, but before the angle levelled out we were soaked and sore from continuous falls. Dark cliffs walled in the tiny lake with the primeval vegetation thickly clustered around the water's edge. The lake itself was still; not a breath of air stirred. The water was black as if frozen solid. The whole scene was like a tableau of a painting by le Douanier Rousseau: a fantastical jungle where I could imagine bizarre animals peering out of the tangle of green foliage.

The little Kitandara hut was almost hidden in the greenery near the water's edge and, for me, it did not come too soon. I had been feeling light-headed and was developing a splitting headache since leaving the pass. Severe nausea meant that I was now suffering from a bout of mountain sickness. Taking just over three days to ascend 10,000 feet was obviously not enough to fully acclimatize me. The other two were not affected, although they had never been even nearly as high as the Freshfield Pass, while I had had several seasons in the high Alps. Altitude sickness is unpredictable, as is attested to in mountaineering literature and mountain guide-books. It could happen equally to the fit and to the unfit; to the experienced climber and to the novice, and indeed at any height much above the one normally lived in. I managed to crawl into a bunk and curl up in my sleeping bag before the more severe bouts of nausea took over. It was worse than a bad dose of seasickness or food poisoning. I remembered that, a few years previously, one climber in the Ruwenzori had died after an attack of altitude sickness. In my misery I felt that this would be a better option for me.

An almost sleepless night followed and by morning I was in no condition to lead the others for an attempt on Mount Baker. As I lay there, slowly recovering, Ralph told me that he had paid off eight of the porters, who were scheduled to return at this point, and that the weather had closed in with visibility down to a few yards. This was a slight consolation to me, since at least my malaise was not the sole cost of a wasted day. That evening I managed to eat a little and hoped that the morning would bring better weather and my recovery.

We were up well before dawn. The sky was clear and we could see that the mist had retreated all the way up to the pass. Feeling well and ready, I proposed an early start, hoping for a further clearance by the time we reached the start of the ridge for Baker. It was still dark as we stumbled by torchlight to the base of the 1,000-foot climb back to the top of the Freshfield Pass. Unlike our horrible descent, the ground was now hard, with frost sparkling on every plant. It was a joy to kick steps into the frozen moss and rotten vegetation and find a secure footing. We gained height rapidly and arrived at the

MOUNT STANLEY

top of the pass at dawn, just as the clouds lifted and the morning sun flooded over the peaks of Mount Stanley.

It was an exhilarating sight to have Sella's panorama laid out before us, but this time in colour. The Stanley plateau was a dazzling white bowl with its surrounding peaks set against an intense blue sky, the main glacier spilling out down over the rocks to the deep valley. The savage black buttresses of Savoia and Elena peaks enclosed the plateau on the east, and away to the west were our main objectives, the twin tallest summits of Alexandra and Margherita: magnificent cones of shining snow and ice soaring above the jagged massif.

It was time to move. We had a long way to go and I was filled with a sense of urgency and anxiety since clouds were beginning to form over the tops of the big summits. I was determined to climb this peak and we had a good chance now; later, bad weather could prevent any further ascents. I was also unsure about George: he was distinctly unenthusiastic and his slowness was holding us back, with the clouds beginning to wreath down from the top. The frozen moss on the rocks helped our progress up to the first snows which brought us out on to the south ridge. I was just able to glimpse where our possible route lay, before the clouds rolled from the valley, boiling up the great corries and burying us in a thick mist.

We kicked steps up a long snow slope and arrived out on the crest. The mist thinned and we were presented with an 80-foot long arête, a sharp snow ridge. George baulked at attempting this. I persuaded him that all that was needed was a steady step and that he would be in the centre of the rope and therefore quite safe. He reluctantly agreed and slowly and clumsily completed what was a fairly simple and easy exercise in snow climbing. I was convinced now that he had little or no mountaineering experience and certainly no skill and was afraid that he was likely to be a severe liability on the climbs.

The arête ended with a small snow cornice that I cut through easily but then, a mixed slope of snow and rock ended with a short vertical drop. I realized that I would have real problems getting George down this, so I tried to find a way to avoid the rock. A steep snow slope on one side offered a way around the obstacle and again I persuaded George to attempt the crossing, while Ralph and I anchored him at each end. After I had cut large steps in the snow, he inched across while I steeled myself for a possible fall. I told him not to look down and, with continual coaxing, he joined me at a safe spot. Ralph rapidly and efficiently joined us and I could relax. A little snow col followed and we came out on to the summit of Edward peak, at 15,988 feet, the highest summit of Mount Baker.

As if on cue, the clouds parted and we had another brief view of the major peaks all the way to Mount Speke, our final goal. We were highly elated at our first success and agreed that, at least, we could return without too much disappointment, like so many others in the past. We were intrigued to find a small metal box half-buried in the neat summit cairn that the Duke of Abruzzi expedition had built. It contained notebook pages with names that were too faded to read and we wondered if this was also the work of those early explorers. We added our names and the date, feeling like pioneers.

The descent was a nightmare: George went from states of panic to stubborn mulishness. I vowed, inwardly, that I would not take him on any other climb: he was a danger to himself as well as to us. By dint of holding him on a tight rope and more coaxing, we overcame the main difficulties and made it on to safer ground. Ralph remained his usual patient self. The snow slope was now softening and the typical Ruwenzori mist enveloped us again. Before we reached the end of the ridge, it began to snow heavily and the descent to the pass over slippery moss-covered rocks was miserable and grim. Our easy morning climb up from the lake now turned into a descent of hellish torment. Boots slid helplessly on the mud and snow-covered vegetation and we took endless falls before the slope flattened out. Then at last, through the thick mist, we could hear the porters calling to us from the lake. We had been out for over twelve hours and, after some hot food, slept for a further twelve.

It rained heavily in the night and when darkness turned into a cold dawn, the visibility was again almost nil. As we contemplated the gloomy scene, the rain turned to snow. It snowed relentlessly for several hours and we gave up all thought of moving. Looking out at the huge flakes floating down on the black waters of the lake, I wondered if our lucky break of the day before would come again. The day's rest would be good for us, I reasoned, so we busied ourselves cleaning our equipment and trying to dry our clothes. The porters, on the other hand, were only too happy to sit around, smoking cigarettes, laughing and chatting. This enforced confinement, however, did not appeal to me for long and I was driven to activity. The snow had stopped and when I went outside I found the landscape transformed into black and white. The cloud lifted a little to reveal that above about 14,000 feet every slope was covered thickly in fresh snow, while in the valley the strange plant forms were even more bizarre, tipped in white mantles. I pushed up through melting slush to a smaller upper lake and for a brief few moments the clouds partly blew away. The terrific boilerplate crags of Baker loomed out of the vapour and cataracts flooded down every gully. The returning wet cold mist ended the drama and I returned to the warm fug of the hut.

The next morning was equally grim: it had rained heavily again in the night and streams were roaring everywhere, but at least the lower snows had vanished. I reasoned that we could not stay at Kitandara any longer and argued that we should at least make an attempt to get higher up to the Elena Glacier where we could wait for our chance to make a quick dash for the summit of Mount Stanley. The others agreed, although George showed little enthusiasm. The porters were reluctant to move, however, and it took an hour's persuasive talk by Wambali before they would pick up their loads and face out into the chilly damp morning.

It was 10 am when the party started up the final slopes to the top of the Scott Elliot Pass. We had been warned to watch out for the possibility of stonefalls from the cliffs of Baker, as the only feasible route went close to the south wall of the mountain. We passed under the danger area quickly, but the visibility diminished again to a few yards. The porters kept losing the track, which anyway was hardly identifiable. Wambali kept screaming at them and they screamed back. We eventually passed up through the vegetation belt and were now out on the moss-covered rocks that led across to the snout of the glacier. It started to snow again and in a short time I realized that we were completely lost on this vast area of slabs. We regrouped and I conferred with Wambali. The conditions were horrible; most of the porters were still in their bare feet and I was sure that they would refuse to go on. To my surprise there was no protest. Instead, they sat on a rock and cheerfully shared a cigarette. We eventually agreed to have one last effort to find the bivouac hut, which, we were told, was sited just below the edge of the plateau.

After another hour we halted and, peering into the drifting snow, we were about to call off the attempt and retreat when, suddenly, in a gap in the mist, a tent-like shape appeared just ahead. The porters dropped their loads and, after extra cigarettes were distributed, tore off with whoops of joy back towards the pass. We arranged with Wambali that

KITANDARA LAKE

we would meet him and a couple of porters on the top of the Scott Elliot Pass on the evening of the next day, or the day after if we did not succeed on our first attempt on the high summits. When the headman disappeared into the mist, we turned to inspect our refuge. A triangular-shaped wooden structure was just high enough for a person to stand in upright in the middle. There was barely room for the three of us to lie flat; otherwise, we could sit with heads bowed. The only daylight came from a small window let into the door. It was shelter from the awful cold and damp outside, however, and with a primus going to melt snow for water, followed by mugs of hot tea, we relaxed for the first time since leaving the lake. The shelter was anchored to the rocks on a narrow shelf beside the glacier and, although nothing was visible we could imagine the tremendous drop into the valley we had left that morning. There were a few breaks at evening and we had a glimpse of the summit of Baker floating above the clouds. The temperature that night dropped to below freezing. We were now above 14,600 feet – as high as the summit of the Matterhorn.

Dawn was 6 am when, after an extremely uncomfortable night, I looked out through the door to see dense mist and swirling snow. It was still snowing, but now more heavily, three hours later, and we abandoned any thought of a quick attack on the summit. All around us was white and silent, except for the whisper of slides from the roof. We felt isolated. The day that followed was far from one of my best days on a mountain. I had often been stranded in high alpine huts, waiting for the weather to improve and, back home, many days and nights were spent sheltering in tents and mountain shacks. The good humour and bantering of friends made these forced sojourns as much fun as a day out climbing. Looking at my two companions of the previous night, I wistfully recalled snuggling up to Nuala in our double sleeping bag in times past when the state of the weather was far from our minds. Ralph had retreated into his most silent self and was sitting reading a damp and tattered paperback, and George was looking even more miserable than usual. I wondered how I would stick twenty-four more hours of this and began to think about those lighthouse keepers, cocooned also in small spaces.

At midday I could stand the confinement no longer and decided to try to reconnoitre a route to the plateau. This could save time, if the weather improved in the morning for a real attempt on the summit. There was a slight break in the mist and the snow had stopped. I said I would go alone and the others did not disagree. The glacier was reached in minutes and the easy angle allowed for fast progress upwards, but I had hardly gone a couple of hundred yards when the thick cloud closed in again. I abandoned the attempt. In the late afternoon there was a much bigger break in the clouds and I made another solo essay by a different route. A snow gully behind the bivouac gave a more direct route up to scattered rocks that were quickly surmounted and I found myself standing on the Stanley plateau. The cloud was right down to the floor of the plateau and all the peaks were enveloped. I sat on a rock, listening to the rumble of avalanches off Margherita.

Finding a wild place to be alone has always provided a

solace for me. On the hill behind my family home, there was a little rocky eyrie to which I would often escape as a boy, when family tensions were too much to bear. These memories came back to me as I sat there in this wildest of places. Soft mist surrounded me again and a light snow was falling gently. Somewhat restored, I climbed back down to the refuge and resigned myself to another endless night of waiting.

Up at 6 am, I saw a clear sky and the long yellow-red line of dawn on the horizon. I made tea and roused the others and by 7 am we were kicking steps up the frozen snow gully. We roped up early, even though the difficulty of the route hardly warranted it, but I was taking no chances with George. The upper rocks were thinly glazed with ice but we bypassed up little snow chutes and quickly overcame the last obstacle, stepping out on to the plateau. The sight was overwhelming and we stood in silence to absorb a scene of spectacular beauty. The rising sun lit the huge expanse of snow to a dazzling white but the outstanding vision was the twin high summits of Mount Stanley, Alexandra and Margherita: pure white towers, domed and crowned with gleaming ice.

It was time to move on. The capricious weather could change in minutes and we would never have a better chance to reach the summit. The way across the plateau, or upper glacier as it really was, looked clear and smooth, but I knew that the recent snowfalls could cover a maze of crevasses. It was time to strap on crampons and move off cautiously, George in the middle. I was the only one with experience of glacier-crossing and went in front, probing with my ice axe wherever I felt that a crack might be hidden. After some slow and tentative starts and stops, we moved at a more steady and confident pace and arrived at the base of Alexandra without incident.

Up close, the final tower was a sublime ice sculpture, fractured and fretted like some fantasy Gothic cathedral. Frozen waterfalls of huge icicles and stalactites seemed to bar the way, and higher up, a series of shining cornices dripped delicate lace curtains of ice. This was rime ice, formed when moisture-laden air froze at this altitude. It was a stunning display, unlike anything experienced before but we still had to find a way to that elusive top.

The early sections were easy and when we emerged on to a wide, almost flat, ledge of snow underneath the first fearsome wall of huge icicles, George announced that he could go no further. He said that he was developing mountain sickness, but it was obvious that the climb was too much for him. I was relieved, since I had already resolved to take him no farther. We suggested that he could safely stay where he was and wait for our return. There was no danger of avalanches, and the morning sun was warm. We left him sitting on his rucksack, looking relieved and more cheerful than he had been for days. I moved around to the left of the wall of icicles where there was a steep slope of solid ice. While Ralph belayed me, I carefully began this first section of serious climbing. I had always enjoyed chopping steps in ice and frozen snow and was soon over the first hurdle. Ralph joined me effortlessly and I was glad of his unruffled support. We pushed on, by way of a very insecure-looking snow bridge over a *bergschrund*, a deep cleft where the snow slope broke away from the cliff above. A steep climb led us to underneath another great cornice, this one laced with icicles and horizontal feathery fronds like giant eyebrows. We were brought to an abrupt halt: it looked impossible to climb.

Carefully working our way around to one side of the cornice, we found that we were looking straight down the stupendous Congo face of the mountain. It looked frightening, but a traverse across the upper section was a possibility, by way of a tiny steep snowfield. We discussed this and Ralph agreed that we should try, because a retreat when we were so near success would be hard to bear. The weather had been changing for some time and clouds flowed quickly over from the west and a thin mist now settled around us. Ralph anchored his axe firmly and began paying out the rope to me. I inched around an icy corner out on to the exposed snowfield. The mist now partly obscured the fearsome drop, but I almost held my breath with tension until I was safe on the other side. Ralph again was steady and calm but he had to agree that it was frightening. Minutes later, mixed snow and rock brought us on to the summit of Alexandra: at 16,703 feet, the highest either of us had ever been.

The clouds below us on the southern side tore away and for a few moments we were staring into an abyss. It was like a bottomless, dark pit, as if we were standing on the edge of the world. We were looking down on the immense forests of the Congo that stretched 1,500 miles to the Atlantic. We stood in silence, exchanging neither words nor handshakes, as if intruders in this high frozen world.

It darkened as the clouds coiled in again and we were enclosed in a clammy fog. The twin summit of Margherita, which was 60 feet higher than Alexandra, was invisible. It was impossible to reach it from where we stood since huge overhanging cornices barred the way to the saddle between the twin peaks. It was cold now: a freezing chill that instilled a sense of dread. The urge to leave this place took charge and we steeled ourselves for the descent.

This was the most dangerous time: euphoria follows success, but complacency can kill. There could be no relaxation until we reached safe ground. Ralph went first, traversing back across that airy snowfield, and now the mist was so dense that he disappeared, with only the rope slowly snaking out to show that he was still moving. It felt strange and unsettling to be alone up there: there was no wind and the silence was total. It was a huge relief to hear Ralph call from the far side of the traverse that he was across and ready for me to join him. This time the crossing seemed less frightening since the dense cloud was hiding the horrific drop. We had to be careful now to locate and follow the exact line of our ascent. The way had been clear earlier but now we were staring into a blanket of vapour.

We gradually inched down, watching out for the scrapes and point marks of our ascent route in the hard snow and ice. It was critical that we stay with this faint trace since losing it could be disastrous. I pushed away the thought of blundering around finding dead ends over strange cornices and, instead, concentrated on finding each indented mark. The *bergschrund* and the rickety snow bridge appeared and we were glad to see the clear line of our earlier steps. Above the last cornice we called out to George and, before the echoes died away, heard his reply and knew that all was well.

He cut a lonely figure sitting there in the swirling mist but was obviously hugely relieved to see us, as indeed were

Ralph and I to find him secure and well. Both of us admitted to feeling guilty at deserting him. The remainder of the way down to the glacier was easy and, since the snow was softening, we could take off the restricting crampons and glissade, or slide down, with abandon.

A rising wind swept away the clouds and blinding sunshine flooded out over the snowfields. The tops of the twin peaks were still shrouded but the whole of the Stanley plateau was now clear. The rear of the plateau was walled in by a long ridge of rock and snow, culminating in the summit of Moebius, at 16, 100 feet. It was still well before noon; the day was fine and the temptation to collect another summit was strong. So far we had been lucky, where many others had been frustrated by continuous bad weather.

'Let's take in Moebius', I said. Ralph agreed at once, but George looked dubious. I told him that he should try it and that it looked feasible and would be a consolation prize for him. I knew, inwardly, that I was easing my conscience for my earlier abandonment of him.

I could hardly hold myself back from charging across the glacier: a glorious day; a gentle wind and I could already see an obvious way of ascent. We still, however, had to be wary of crevasses, so our progress was frustratingly slow, at least to me, impatient to succeed again. A gently angled snow gully led up to a wide ridge that straddled the Uganda-Congo border. Progress along this was fast, and the final hurdle was to surmount a jumble of rocks with just one difficult section. Here I was in my element — dry, firm rock, warm to the touch: I shouted for joy. The others followed easily and George wore a broad grin when he stood on the summit.

We lingered a while, savouring the pleasure of success and enjoying the first hot sun after days of damp and cold. The gods of the mountain soon decided we had had enough and the clouds descended again. We followed our footprints back along the ridge and down the snow gully to the glacier. I managed to get a fix on Baker summit in a brief gap in the mist before we set off to reach the Elena bivouac. We still had not encountered a single serious crevasse, but I was concerned that the recent heavy snowfalls had covered over any sign of fracture. I took extra care, prodding at any suspicious wrinkle. In addition, a straight line bearing had to be followed so as to strike the plateau's edge at the right point. We made a perfect landfall, arriving exactly above the little hut, just as snow began to fall once more.

We hurriedly packed up, stuffing everything into and on top of rucksacks and set of at speed to cross the rock slabs to the Scott Elliot Pass where we hoped to find porters waiting for us. The visibility was now almost nil, with thickly falling flakes making it difficult to see. It was necessary to drop a couple of hundred feet and then contour to the lip of the pass. Losing precious height and having to struggle up again, while exhausted, was a climber's nightmare. Our voices must have been heard, for Wambali called out and we were able easily to traverse to the top of the pass. Three porters took our sacks and we thankfully continued unencumbered down the thickly vegetated slopes to the Bujuku valley. The little timber hut loomed out of the gathering dusk: a welcome sight. The porters had a fire going under the nearby rock shelter and, jaded now, we were soon lulled into a snug torpor by the soft roar of our primus stove and the warm glow of candles.

Dawn came to a valley transformed. The sky was blue and every vestige of cloud and vapour had vanished. Frost sparkled on each spiky plant and rounded mossy rock, while all around us the three main massifs of Baker, Stanley and Speke shone clear in the early sun. The Vittorio Emmanuel peak, the highest summit of Mount Speke, was our last objective and on that splendid morning it looked as if all our plans would succeed. We took time to study the possible route to the summit since, for once, a clear view opened all the way from the valley. The normal ascent, we had been told, was from the top of the Stuhlmann Pass and then more or less directly to the highest point. There were two glaciers visible, the Speke and the Johnston, which ran down from the skyline, separated by a jumble of shattered ice. We decided to try the normal route.

George announced that he had had enough and would not go with us. I was relieved since I had already decided not to take him: my toleration for coaxing and cajoling had run out. Ralph and I made a good team; he was steady and uncomplaining, a necessary calming influence on my more driven ambitions.

We set off in high spirits but, worryingly, when the climb to the pass began, clouds were already forming on all the summits. The early frost had melted and the gullies leading up to the Stuhlmann Pass soon became rivers of liquid mud and rotting vegetation. After more than an hour's struggle, the slope eased and we assumed that we had reached the top of the pass, but the thickening cloud obscured all landforms that could point to possible routes. A loom of rising ground on our right tempted us onwards, but we were soon engaged in an even more desperate struggle, with further steep slopes of mud and slippery vegetation. There was no sign of any feasible line and the mist prevented us from spotting an alternative.

It was time to confer. Ralph and I were in agreement that it was hopeless, as well as being unenjoyable, to continue on our present course and that we would either try some very different line or else give up. I suggested that since this was our last possible climb, we make one more effort to find a way. Ralph, as always, concurred, but this time I wondered if I might be pushing him, as well as myself, too far. In that early morning's clear light I had taken careful note of the glaciers, Speke and Johnston. The tongues of each were more or less in line with the top of the Stuhlmann Pass and I calculated that if we traversed the slope we could reach the start of the ice, thus avoiding futile battles up the mud gullies. The glaciers might then present a possible ascent line: the Johnston looked the more feasible of the two, from the morning inspection. 'Anything must be better than this,' said Ralph. The decision was made.

Contouring was easy and we quickly saw the first dirt-stained snouts of the glacier, but which one? We had seen that the Speke had a nasty ice-fall at its foot, while the Johnston was more gradually inclined. Visibility was still limited to about 50 yards so we had to take a chance. We strapped on crampons and I led up the first tongues of ice: a pleasure after the horrendous mud. An ice-fall soon faced us but it appeared to be stable and well inclined from vertical. There was, however, a maze of crevasses and we had to range widely, zigzagging to find a way. Suddenly a steep snow slope appeared and we were past the worst. As if on cue, the sun broke through and the panorama of the mountains was revealed. Away to our right, many minor peaks floated over a sea of dark green, with the glaciers of Mount Emin and Mount Gessi spotlessly white against a blue sky.

Up on the ridge we could see that we had climbed the Johnston glacier, avoiding the more hazardous Speke. The sun was now scorching and the snow glare was blinding, making goggles essential. The final walk along the ridge and up easy rocks and snow to the summit of Vittorio Emmanuel, at 16,042 feet, was pure pleasure, the morning's battle forgotten.

It was a sublime experience on this gentler summit, high above the Equator and all around us a pristine wilderness. We allowed ourselves to linger, on this our last climb, so as to fully savour our success. Ralph's usual reticence yielded a little and we indulged each other in self-congratulatory chat.

It was time to go. We started down the normal route, although we had only vague information as to its where-abouts, but when it began to mist up again, we halted. The consequences of committing ourselves to an unknown way were serious. If we veered off the correct line to the pass, we could end up down in the unmapped wilderness on the Congo side and be truly lost. The best option was to retrace our steps and reverse our glacier route. Back on the summit, the clouds closed in and it began to snow. We raced down the ridge, hoping our early footprints were not covered. Visibility was now down to a few yards, but our prints were still clear when we reached the turn-off point for the glacier descent. The steep snow slope was easy but the ice-fall conditions were now terrible. The early morning freeze-up had changed to soggy soft snow; we both, separately, fell into crevasses when bridges collapsed. Fortunately each fall was checked by quick ropework.

The mist lifted: we cleared the end of the ice and emerged on to the rocky upper slopes. Unroping, I promptly slid down a moss-covered slab after relaxing my concentration for a moment. My fall was halted in a clump of rotten lobelia and the result was torn trousers and a few minor cuts. We reached the hut, bruised and battered, but supremely happy. We had emulated Tilman and Shipton but, more importantly, felt privileged to be, for even a little while, in this wondrous place.

That night it was time to celebrate. The bottle of whisky, which we had brought for the purpose had, miraculously, survived the long carry. The porters were already celebrating around a fine fire under the rock overhang: their laughter was uproarious, and tales, no doubt, were being told. I'm sure we figured in the stories. The *bwanas* were less ebullient, but the successful end of the adventure gave each of us, even George, quiet satisfaction. The release of tension after a safe return from the heights was one of the attractions of climbing and, paradoxically, the return to the valley from the enchanted hills was always a delicious prospect.

At one stage our relaxed chat turned to the names of these great mountains. It seemed perverse that every single main peak was named after a European – either an explorer or royalty. The minor peaks, all below the snow line, had African names: was this an inanimate colour bar? The Duke of Abruzzi named the mountains after he returned from his famous expedition of 1906. It was understandable that at a time when European powers were empire-building by whole-sale land-grabbing in Africa, the hierarchy of white over black was taken for granted. The three main massifs were named after three great explorers but the summits of these were given to royalty; Italian mainly but, as a sop to the British, Edward and Alexandra. There was one odd exception to this overwhelming European nomenclature in that Mount Speke had an alternative African name – Duwoni – which was marked on our primitive map. None of us had ever heard or seen it used.

A fresh outbreak of naming occurred as late as 1953, after the coronation of Queen Elizabeth II and the nationalistic fervour that followed the British team's ascent of Everest. A small glacier on Mount Stanley was designated the Corona-tion, and two minor summits were given the names Elizabeth and Philip. This seemed to me extremely insensitive, given that self-government for Uganda had already been agreed for the end of the decade. There was some dissension in the Mountain Club about this action and, to make amends, it was proposed that two minor points on the Stanley massif be given more appropriate names of local origin. The names chosen were Kitasamba, a mythological deity of the Bakonjo, and Nyabubuya, his wife.

These gods smiled on us the next morning. We were up just before dawn to a clear sky and fading stars. The first sun touched the white tops and warm light flooded over the glaciers. The Bujuku valley opened out before us, with every rocky peak and serrated ridge sharp against an intense blue sky. The floor of the valley was dotted with giant lobelias, their spiky heads shining green with stems sprouting tall from the yellowing tussock grass. In the centre of the valley the black waters of Lake Bujuku mirrored the snowfields high above. The cirque was walled in on three sides by the highest mountains of the Ruwenzori. The savage dark buttresses of Mount Baker faced the bright ice slopes of Mount Speke, with the centre dominated by the huge mass of Mount Stanley and its twin gleaming summits, Alexandra and Margherita.

We turned to go; loads packed; the porters already racing off, but it was hard not to pause and gaze for the last time at the spectacle.

Our return route would follow the Bujuku river until it merged with the Mobuku, where we would rejoin our earlier ascent trail, thus completing a circular tour of the region's highest peaks. We made rapid time, except for the crossing of the notorious Bigo bogs. All the headwaters of the Bujuku seemed to spread out on this flat plain and sluggishly stagnate. The result was an entropic canopy of tussock floating on a sea of ooze. Even the porters, whose loads were now considerably lighter, gave loud yelps of exasperation as we slithered and squelched from unsteady tussock to knee-deep quagmire.

The day was still fine and the peaks still visible, whenever we glanced behind, as we left the horrible bogs and pushed on a long way down the river to the rock shelter and tiny hut at Nyamleju. We were now a day late from our scheduled return, as a result of the bad weather and delay on Mount Stanley. Ralph and I had to be back at work, and George, at this stage, was concerned only that his agony would end. I suggested that we attempt a double march the next day to reach the road head and recover lost time. Wambali said that the porters would agree: they were eager to get back to family

LAKE BUJUKU AND MOUNT STANLEY

and friends and, not least, their final pay and bonus. Ralph, as usual, was game to try and George had no option but to agree.

The weather still held for our final day. We had one last glimpse of the snows of the Equator before the lower peaks closed off the view. We started early since the porters were afraid of the elephants in the forest. Passing below the Nyinabitaba hut, we crossed over the junction with the

Mobuku and were back on the final stretch to Ibanda.

The villagers gave the party an ecstatic welcome; the last *shillingi* were distributed; unused supplies were accepted as gifts and prolonged farewells ended only as we drove away.

A friend, Ronnie Wathen, poet and climber, following his expedition to the Andes in 1956, wrote: 'Sometimes it seems as if we expect too much of the mountains. We seek, as it were, a heaven on earth, a lifetime of happiness in the single flush of an alpine dawn. When we do not find this heaven, we are disenchanted, like a man tired in middle age. . . . We forget that it is the intensity of the experience, not its duration that counts – its quality, not its quantity. We return to the valleys, tired of the mountains – surfeited.

But suddenly we must return. We have got safely off our last mountain. But always we must return. We must go back to the white mountains, like moths returning to the flame of a candle.'

CHAPTER 7

THE WHITE NILE

At the head of the Bujuku valley small streams flow down the flanks of Mount Speke, converging to drain into tiny Lake Bujuku.

THE HIGHEST OF THESE is born from the melting ice of the glacier and must be the true source of the Nile. The waters from these wild highlands make an extraordinarily circuitous journey around the massif of the Ruwenzori to where the outfalls from the two great lakes, Albert and Victoria, merge to become the White Nile.

John Hanning Speke first claimed to have discovered the source of the Nile in 1858 when he reached the southern shore of a vast inland lake, hitherto unknown to Europeans: naming it Victoria, in honour of his monarch. The expedition that set out from Zanzibar in 1857 to explore the interior of Africa was a joint venture between two men whose characters were so different from each other that they were polar opposites. Richard Burton was an adventurer and a considerable scholar, unorthodox and volatile, a romantic and a libertine. Speke was a rigid Victorian, quiet and abstemious, but with a determination to carry a project through to the end. Both men had been officers in the Indian Army and their courage was without question.

Their first discovery was Lake Tanganyika, where Burton's theory that this was the source of the Nile was squashed: the main river flowed into the lake instead of out. The pair split here and Speke went north, following on some scrappy local rumour of another great lake. When he arrived on the southern shore, he failed to explore farther and establish the extent of his find. Instead, he returned to Burton and announced that he had discovered the great river's source. Burton ridiculed his claim and, not for the first time, relations between the two cooled.

Both men became seriously ill on the punishing return journey but, when they arrived returned to the coast, Speke had recovered sufficiently to travel home to England. Burton needed time to convalesce and thought that they had agreed to delay publicity about the expedition until both were united in London. Speke was hardly back home when he announced his discovery. He was lionized as a great explorer and invited by the Royal Geographical Society to lead a new expedition. This one was to explore the northern shores of Speke's discovery and settle, once and for all, the source of the Nile and the existence of the Mountains of the Moon.

Burton arrived back in England to find that he was an almost forgotten figure and was not invited to join Speke on the new adventure. A bitter enmity was born.

Speke's partner for the new venture was a Captain James Grant. Another Indian Army officer, Grant was the ideal companion: willing and subservient and somewhat in awe of his leader. The expedition set out from Zanzibar in late 1860 but took more than a year to reach Lake Victoria. After crossing several rivers flowing into the lake, Speke finally arrived on the banks of the Nile. In his *Journal of the Discovery of the Source of the Nile* he describes his first view of the river:

> Here at last I stood on the brink of the Nile; most beautiful was the scene, nothing could surpass it! It was the very perfection of the kind of effect aimed at in a highly kept park; with a magnificent stream from 600 to 700 yards wide, dotted with islets and rocks, the former occupied by fishermen's huts, the latter by sterns [birds] and crocodiles basking in the sun … flowing between fine grassy banks, with rich trees and plantains in the background, where herds of the nsunnu [gnu] and hartebeest could be seen grazing, while the hippopotami were snorting in the water.

At this point Speke was still some 40 miles from the actual outlet of the river from the lake: after a week's march upstream, he came on the magnificent falls where the full force of the Nile cascades out of the great inland sea. He named these the Ripon Falls, 'after the nobleman who presided over the Royal Geographical Society when my expedition was got up.' He then announced triumphantly: 'The expedition had now performed its functions. I saw that old father Nile without doubt rises in the Victoria N'yanza, and, as I had foretold, that lake is the great source of the holy river which cradled the first expounder of our religious belief.'

Speke's hubris here may have been understandable but was to cost him dearly. On his return to England, his initial reception was tumultuous; 'The Nile is settled,' he announced to an overflow audience at a special meeting of the Royal Geographical Society, but Burton was waiting to pounce. He scorned his rival's claims; Speke had not followed the river downstream along its banks to prove that the glimpses he had seen were all of the same waterway; he had not circumnavigated the great lake to prove it was one big body of water and not several and, in any case, rivers do not originate from lakes but from highlands. The seeds of doubt were sown.

Supporters of Burton initiated a vicious campaign to denigrate Speke, to the extent that some published rants against him were libellous. To try to settle the matter, a debate was arranged a year after Speke's expedition had returned to England. It was to be hosted by the British Association for the Advancement of Science at Bath. The rivals were each to present their respective theories before a distinguished audience of scientists and geographers. On the morning before the debate was due to start, it was announced that Speke was dead. Apparently he had been out shooting on his estate the previous day and, when climbing over a stone wall, his gun had gone off and he was shot in the chest. Was it an accident or did he commit suicide, rather than face Burton in the debate? This was never satisfactorily resolved.

In some ways both men were right. Speke had discovered Lake Victoria and certainly the greatest body of water flowed out over the Ripon Falls, but all rivers do have their genesis in the highlands.

Each of the eminent African explorers has been celebrated in the naming of great peaks and landmarks. Speke has not alone a magnificent mountain and a glacier named after him but also, less flatteringly I suppose, a hotel. Grant, however, was so self-effacing that, unlike most of his contemporaries in Africa, he is celebrated only by a street – Grant Street, our office address in Kampala. Uniquely, however, of all these remarkable explorers, Burton's name is nowhere to be seen. Victorian prudery and disapproval of his lifestyle and his espousal of erotic eastern writings put paid, perhaps, to a Mount Burton alongside Stanley, Speke, Baker, Luigi Di Savoia, Emin and Gessi.

One of our earliest excursions outside of Kampala was to view the source of the Nile. The fine tarmac road to Jinga made this an easy Sunday outing through a landscape of dense forest, interspersed with high papyrus swamps and wooded hillocks. There was little or no open country and any cleared forest was filled with thick groves of banana plantations. Mile after mile of this lush intense greenery gave way at last to the astonishing vista of the great river. It was easy to imagine the emotions of Speke when he looked out over the roaring waters and knew that the ultimate prize was his: he was the first European to add tangible detail to Ptolemy's map of Africa circa A.D. 150. That famous ancient geographer was also correct: the Nile did flow out of a great lake, while it, in turn, was fed by waters from the Lunae Montes.

The 'roar of the waters', as described by Speke, was, however, no longer to be heard. The recently built Owen Falls Dam was Uganda's first major hydroelectric scheme, bringing the territory into the modern world. The level of the water upstream of the dam had now risen to eliminate the falls, but it was still a strangely overwhelming experience to stare out at the enormous rush of almost silent water, beginning its over 4,000-mile journey to the Mediterranean. On a rocky islet in the stream cormorants rested, wings outstretched, while terns swooped and dived. A long-legged golden crested crane stood in the shallows: the supremely elegant symbol of Uganda.

Speke's plan was to follow the Nile downstream until he could link up with a rescue expedition that had been prearranged to move upriver with boats from Khartoum. These would be used to ferry the explorers back to Egypt and thence to England. There had been rumours of another great lake to the west, the Luta Nzigé, and Speke was anxious to see if this could be another source of the Nile. This unmapped wilderness that Speke had traversed was now a new national park and we were determined to visit it.

The Murchison Falls was almost 200 miles from Kampala: all but the last fifty on a reasonable road. It was a long way for our tiny Fiat, but after nearly two years in Uganda we felt confident to undertake a proper safari in our own car. This time our friend Carmel joined us for the trip and, with toddler Eoin, we had little room for luggage. Here in the tropics, however, our needs were few: the shallow space under the bonnet of the Fiat sufficed for storage. Water was always a problem, and we invariably carried a tin or canvas sack. The last settlement before the wilderness began was Masindi in Bunyoro province and we made good progress through a rolling savannah of wide, sweeping grasslands. At one point, several hours after leaving the forests around Kampala, we saw a low dark cloud across the horizon in front. We hoped this was not a storm since the short rains were forecast and this could make some minor roads impassable.

As we drove nearer, the cloud turned out to be smoke. There was a slow-moving line of fire in a huge semi-circle over the plain. It did not appear very menacing and we stopped to have a look. Walking out to the edge of the blaze we saw a herd of eland leaping off to safety. The flames were only a few inches high and were slowly eating away at the yellow grass but giving off dense smoke. A couple of spindly thorn trees were black and still crackling in the heat. Our thought was that lightning may have started the fire and when we passed through the last vestige of smoke, we saw far-off flickers of white in a darkening sky.

Leaving Masindi, we started out into the wilderness: fifty miles of winding dirt track lay ahead before we would reach the banks of the Nile and the Rest Camp at Murchison. Our initial anxiety about the weather turned to real concern. The sky to the east was now a blue-black mass of boiling clouds and it seemed as if a storm would break at any minute. We crossed numerous fords over watercourses, but there was still no sign of rain and the beds of the streams were dry, with not a trickle of water to be seen. The sky brightened again and sunshine flooded over the landscape as we slowly and carefully steered to avoid deep ruts in the iron-hard red surface and then speeded up on short flat gritty stretches. All at once we appeared to be driving along the edge of a deep ravine, which in contrast to the scorched plain was filled with dense greenery. We stopped for a rest and, staring down at the shrubbery, saw a herd of elephants feeding on the leaves. They advanced, almost in slow motion, along the margin of the vegetation, tearing off swathes of branches with their curling trunks and, although only about 50 yards away, paid no attention to us. We took photographs, feeling cocksure about our encounters with wildlife. This was to change minutes later.

Rounding a bend that was hidden by clusters of thorn trees, we almost drove into another family of huge animals standing right in the roadway. We stopped, the engine was switched off and we sat, silent and petrified. More elephants appeared from the thorn thickets until the car was surrounded by what seemed to us was a grey wall of monstrous forms, slowly shifting and weaving. We wound the car windows up carefully and froze. We had been warned by the experts that we should never, ever, try to drive through a family of elephants and sounding the horn would be inviting disaster. Eoin was sitting on Nuala's knee and the horn was always an attraction for him. 'Keep him away', I whispered, clutching the steering. Minutes passed, but it seemed like hours, until the herd, led by two enormous matriarchs, resumed its march across the track. It was a stunning spectacle to watch the slow-moving procession of these majestic creatures whose huge legs seemed to pad noise-lessly in the dust. We sat until the last of the animals, wide ears flapping, had moved well away from the track before we felt safe to start the car and move off.

A mile or so farther on, there was a lone acacia on rising ground and under it a solitary bull elephant stood. He was enormous; his curving tusks almost touched the ground: the picture was a sublime evocation of Africa. There was, somehow, an indefinable feeling of sadness in the posture of that lonely figure, head bowed, his days forever to be spent separated from the bond of family.

The sky had darkened again and to the east the clouds were solid black but, strangely, we still had no rain. It was all the more shocking then to come over a rise in the track and find a roaring torrent barring the way. It was an enormous flash flood – a nightmare of travellers in wild places. It dawned on us that the myriad of watercourses we had just crossed would be inundated and we were now trapped. We looked out at the wide channel of brown rushing water, torn branches swirling along, and saw the top of a pole sticking up from the edge of the flood. It appeared to have been marked off at one-foot intervals; the top mark was 20. The water cascaded past at the mark 17. If the river were now seventeen feet deep, how long would it be before it went down to the level of the ford?

A small round hut was perched nearby on the high ground and when we noticed a similar structure on the far bank, we realized that these were refuges for trapped travellers like ourselves. We were stuck for the night, at least we hoped for only one night: the question was, could that flood recede by the next day? We had a little food but no blankets or bedding and, more seriously, only one small mosquito net, which we had brought for Eoin. The hut was a tiny round space, but roomy enough for all of us. The walls were closely interwoven rods daubed with mud, while the roof was covered with overlapping plantain leaves. The doorway and two windows were just simple openings. We used a car seat as a bed for Eoin and rigged up the mosquito net overhead on a tripod of branches. The two of us had to squat on the floor, backs to the wall, or stretch out on the dirt surface.

It was a long, long night, and we alternatively dozed and jerked awake as something, alive or dead, dropped on to us from above. Earlier we had seen lots of small geckos scuttling up the walls and roof: we hoped that these harmless lizards were the live things touching our bodies and not some poisonous creatures. None of us mentioned snakes, not to speak of night prowling animals and that open doorway. The insects were the worst. All night the mosquitoes whined and I was bitten savagely: we each took our paludrin tablets, but without the protection of nets we could be vulnerable to malaria.

We must have slept a little as birdsong woke us first and the early morning sun was streaming through the open doorway into our refuge. Our initial thought was the river – had it gone down? I looked out over the bank and saw the pole standing almost clear of the water: it was down to the one-foot mark and the stones of the ford were clearly visible. I waded across to test the flow and found that it was still quite strong; enough, possibly, to sweep the lightweight Fiat off course. We decided to wait for an hour or two, the camp being only a few miles away.

It was a long wait: the level came down by only a couple of inches. I was getting impatient and there was always the possibility of another flash flood appearing, even though the sky was clear. I decided to try to cross. Carmel and Nuala, carrying Eoin, waded over to the other side and I eased the car down the steep incline. Then, in first gear with my foot hard on the accelerator, the Fiat bounced and roared over the rocky stream bed and up the far bank, to cheers from the others. The remaining watercourses were mere rivulets and soon we could see the camp, on high ground straight in front.

The Murchison Park Camp was not long established and consisted of a group of large tents pitched in a line along the edge of a high bluff that looked straight down at the Nile. A small stone building stood a little back from the edge and this housed the dining room, kitchen and office of the warden. We had made our reservations in Kampala and were immediately welcomed and shown to our tent. A large A-shaped structure of spindly poles and plaited papyrus was erected over each canvas tent to protect visitors from the heat of the sun, and a timber floor was projected out in front of the opening as a veranda. Simple canvas camp beds had mosquito nets hung from the tent roof and several basket chairs completed the furnishing. Since the tents were high enough for standing, they offered luxury compared to our former nights of cramped mountain camping.

The river was the star turn, however, and the spectacle below us was certainly worth the trials of the journey. The Victoria Nile, as it was known at this point, was a wide waterway, so slow-moving as to resemble a placid lake. Directly in front of us the dark brown backs of dozens of hippos undulated in the water with the occasional gigantic head and open jaws giving that strange guttural sound. Statuesque herons stalked along the shallows, and snow-white egrets flapped on to the backs of the hippos.

The evening meal was timed to allow us to get back to our tents before dark, because, while the hippos or crocodiles did not come up the steep face of the bluff, leopards did roam at night. That first evening we settled back on our veranda to enjoy the sunset, and the African ex-pat ritual of the sundowner drink. As the light faded, a giant form blocked our view: an elephant padded past, followed by a half-dozen others in a stately parade, uncomfortably close to the front of our tent. We were told afterwards that this was often a nightly event. Closing the canvas flaps as darkness fell gave a fragile sense of security when the sounds of the night, for a short while only, kept us awake.

The highlight of the Park experience was the river trip, upstream to the spectacular Murchison Falls. In the early morning our small group assembled on the riverbank. We were joined by a handful of other visitors who, like ourselves, were working in Kampala. Our guide was a leathery-skinned white Kenyan of indeterminate years, whose enthusiasm for the wildlife was infectious. It was slightly disconcerting, however, to see the small size of the boat we were to embark on: an open steel craft with a tiny outboard engine. The swelling mass of hippos was less than 50 yards from our landing place, but our guide assured us that they rarely gave trouble. The 'rarely' information was less reassuring when the boat chugged off in midstream and an occasional enormous head with unblinking huge eyes rose up close alongside, to stare at us.

It was cool out in the middle of the great river and the slow steady glide through the almost still waters allowed us to sit back and relax. The high banks gave way to grassy swards dotted with groves of mimosa and acacias. We floated past groups of elephants, buffalo, zebra, antelope, eland, wildebeest, and warthog. A pair of African darters, or snakebirds as Africans called them, their elegant long necks stretched, were perched on a spindly branch overhanging the water. The sinister scaly backs of crocodiles lay half-submerged and, when a section of sandbank appeared ahead, we could see dozens of log-like shapes scattered over it. At a wide bend and as the boat nosed through a bed of shallow reeds, there was a tremendous splash at the front of the boat and a monstrous crocodile leaped away towards the bank. The guide nonchalantly steered us towards the creature, which now turned to show its open jaws and yellowing teeth. 'The Nile crocodile is the largest in the world', the guide informed us. We were rigid with fright until the boat was back out in the deep.

Suddenly the falls were straight ahead. A white plume arched out of a split black crag and, as the boat sailed nearer, we nosed through carpets of feathery foam. At the foot of the falls we were enveloped in a fine wet mist: all the waters of the Victoria Nile were jetting out of this narrow defile, calmed in the widening lower reaches of the flat, slow-flowing stream. On the way back I thought about Speke. He had followed the river down from the lake, towards this point, but apparently had never seen these falls. He left the river to strike north at the Karuma Falls, which he described as a mere sluice down a ten-foot drop. He then made the casual observation that there were other falls of minor importance 'and one within ear-sound, down the river, said to be very grand'. This certainly could refer to the Murchison but it was still 40 miles away and not within 'ear-sound'. African and European concepts of distance were often at odds.

The three-year expedition of Speke and Grant was near its end and Speke, certainly, was becoming cranky. His frustration with Kamrasi, the king of Bunyoro, through whose territory he had wanted to pass, becomes increasingly evident in his writings. Towards the end of his book, the lofty moral superiority of the Victorian white explorer is loud in this account:

The same evening I was attracted by the sound of drums to a neighbouring village, where, by the moonlight, I found the natives were dancing. A more indecent or savage spectacle I never witnessed. The whole place was alive with naked humanity in a state of constant motion. Drawing near, I found that a number of drums were beaten by men in the centre. Next to them was a deep ring of women, half of whom carried their babies; and outside these again was still deeper circle of men, some blowing horns, but most holding their spears erect. To the sound of the music both these rings of the opposite sexes kept jumping and sidling round and round the drummers, making the most grotesque and obscene motions to one another.

The wholesale slaughter of the wildlife of Africa did not seem to disturb Speke's Victorian sensibilities as much as the recreational activities of the 'natives'. Throughout his book there are continuous references to the shooting of animals and birds. Most of this killing was, of necessity, for the feeding of the expedition, but there are also casual accounts of pot shots at various species, evidently for sport. In one chapter he tells of shooting a zebra and wounding it but then he walks off, presumably leaving it to die. Zebras did not appear to be on the menu for his porters. There is one detailed account of a particularly gory killing where there is an unmistakable air of gratification in the act.

> Shortly after, towards the close of the day's work, as a solitary buffalo was seen grazing by a brook, I put a bullet through him, and allowed the savages the pleasure of dispatching him in their own wild fashion with spears. It was a sight quite worthy of a little delay. No sooner was it observed that the huge beast could not retire, than, with springing bounds, the men, all spear in hand, as if advancing on an enemy, went top speed at him, over rise and fall alike, till, as they neared the maddened bull, he instinctively advanced to meet his assailants with the best charge his exhausted body could muster up. Wind, however, failed him soon; he knew his disadvantage, and tried to hide by plunging in the water – the worst policy he could have pursued, for the men from the bank above him soon covered him with bristling spears, and gained their victory.

THE WHITE NILE AND MURCHISON FALLS

Photography was the only acceptable form of shooting nowadays, we concluded, that evening at the camp, after a discussion about the newly established wildlife parks in East Africa. Looking out through the open doorway of the dining hall, I saw a couple of elephants tearing at the shrubbery nearby.

I grabbed my camera and rushed out to get the perfect picture. In the viewfinder I had a superb close-up and snapped off a few shots, but suddenly one animal's head went down and its huge ears were spread wide and I was faced with a charging beast. I fled back to the refuge of the stone building and then wondered whether or not I had pressed the shutter as the charge began. I had to wait to get back to Kampala and several weeks' delay before my developed film was returned. There it was: the consummate study of a charging elephant and I was still alive. I had been, however, severely scolded by the warden.

The northwestern edge of the Murchison National Park stretches along the banks of the Albert Nile, the second source of the great river. It was Speke's failure to continue his march westward to definitely prove the existence of this other huge lake, the Luta Nzigé, which fuelled the denunciations of his critics. It was understandable, however, that after three years of excruciating hardship he wanted to end the enterprise. By striking directly north, well away from the second great lake and not finding the Nile again for more than another 100 miles, he laid himself wide open to the sneers of his detractors.

He arrived at a place on the river called Gondokoro, to be met by an old friend, Sir Samuel Baker. This formidable character had set out from Khartoum with the stated aim of finding Speke, now thought to be lost in the African wilds. His other hope, however, was that he would be the one who discovered the true source of the Nile. When he heard that the mystery of the location of Luta Nzigé was still unsolved, Baker instantly decided to push south and thus claim his place in the history of exploration of the 'Dark Continent'.

Speke was overjoyed to meet Baker for he realized that his trials were now over and that he could go home. He described how 'my old friend Baker, famed for his sports in Ceylon, seized me by the hand'.

> Baker then said he had come up with three vessels…fully equipped with armed men, camels, horses, donkeys, beads, brass wire, and everything necessary for a long journey, expressly to look after us, hoping, as he jokingly said, to find us on the equator in some terrible fix, that he might have the pleasure of helping us out of it.

Unlike Burton, Grant and Speke, Baker was a civilian and a very wealthy man, well able to fund an extravagant expedition. His sport was shooting big game: tigers, bears, elephants had all fallen to his especially made guns in India and Ceylon and he could therefore be described as East Africa's first 'white hunter'. He was accompanied by his second wife, a beautiful Hungarian, fifteen years his junior. Despite his lavish expedition, his journey south to King Kamrasi's Bunyoro was fraught with danger and disease: the pair had to battle with terrible bouts of malaria. Finally, after more than a year of unimaginable hardship, they reached the shore of the Luta Nzigé, which Baker promptly named Lake Albert. He published an account of the travels of himself and his wife shortly after they returned to Britain. The writing style was much more lively and readable than Speke's often dull, long-winded and ponderous prose. In one quite lyrical passage he describes his arrival, his sick wife standing by his side, on the banks of the fabled Luta Nzigé:

> The day broke beautifully clear, and having crossed a deep valley

between the hills, we toiled up the opposite slope. I hurried to the summit. The glory of our prize burst suddenly upon me! There, like a sea of quicksilver, lay far beneath, the grand expanse of water – a boundless sea horizon on the south and south-west glittering in the noon-day sun; and on the west, at fifty or sixty miles' distance, blue mountains rose from the bosom of the lake to a height of about 7,000 feet above sea level. It is impossible to describe the triumph of that moment; here was reward for all our labour – for the years of tenacity with which we had toiled through the Africa.

They managed to buy some dug-out canoes and laboriously paddled along the lakeshore until they reached the point where the Victoria Nile joined the lake. They then had an easy passage past the site of the present rest camp and thus became the first Europeans to see the magnificent falls: Baker gave himself the privilege of naming these in honour of Sir Roderick Murchison, President of the Royal Geographical Society. On his return to London he was awarded the gold medal of the Society and an inevitable knighthood. He had made a clever choice of names.

It was a lot easier for us, some ninety years later, to follow the winding dirt tracks in the little Fiat to the outfall of that lake, where the waterways of Victoria and Albert merge to create the White Nile. We stood on a rocky bluff and gazed out over the wide expanse of sparkling water. A few puffy white clouds hung in the intensely blue sky, and faraway to the west we could see the faint outlines of hills. On our left a small sandy spit curved out, with three tall euphorbia trees starkly outlined against the glare of the midday sun. It was then that we noticed, just below us, the half-camouflaged head of a crocodile jutting out from the shade. We made a fast retreat to the safety of the car. Just back from the edge of the water someone had stuck the bleached skull of a buffalo on a stick: this invited a photograph of Eoin, held by Nuala and perched between the fearsome S-shaped curved horns.

On our drive back home we passed the site of our earlier enforced benightment to find that the ford was now dry and, shortly after this, the map indicated a track leading towards the top of the Murchison Falls. It was tempting to make this diversion, since it was only about five miles. The early stretches of the trail were lined with high grasses. I had to brake suddenly when a pair of large warthogs, followed by a string of young, shot out from the side and raced ahead of us, before plunging back into cover. Our little car easily managed the looping trail, swerving around fallen debris and sand-filled hollows to bring us out on to the top of a rocky hillock. A thunderous roar nearly deafened us as we scrambled down the craggy slope to near the edge of the gorge. The broad blue waters of the upstream Nile were now forced into a twenty-foot wide sluice and transformed into a tearing white torrent. The black walls of the gorge were framed in a perfect rainbow, lacing through the misty spray. Talk was impossible: the stupendous spectacle was overwhelming.

CHAPTER 8

KARAMOJA

The twin dark peaks of Napak and Akisim, rising from the plain, formed a portal in the distant shimmering haze.

THE ROAD, hardly more than a track, pointed directly towards this gap in the flat, desolate landscape. The police post at Lothaa consisted of a huddle of rondavels – round aluminum huts, covered with grass to insulate the occupants from the searing sun. Watching us from the far side of the track, as we presented our pass documents to the *askari* on duty, were two jet-black naked men, each leaning on a tall spear. A small woman, clad in a nondescript dun-coloured shift and balancing a large bundle on her head, stood nearby. We were entering the territory of Karamoja.

It was our second Christmas in Uganda and a chance to have a short holiday. Everybody said that we must try to take a trip up north to Karamoja; that it was an extraordinary place, inhabited by a warrior tribe, the Karamojong, whose way of life had been unchanged for centuries. We were intrigued, since it sounded as if this was the place where we would encounter the Africa of those early heroic explorers – the real Africa. The enthusiastic endorsements of those who had been there hinted, perhaps, of praise of the 'noble savage', so beloved of Victorian writers.

Karen Blixen's book *Out of Africa*, reissued as a Penguin paperback in 1954, reinforced this romantic, if somewhat patronizing, vision:

> The Natives were Africa in flesh and blood. The tall extinct volcano of Longonot that rises above the Rift Valley, the broad mimosa trees along the rivers, the elephant and the giraffe, were not more truly Africa than the natives were – small figures in an immense scenery. All were different expressions of one idea, variations of the same theme.... We ourselves, in boots, and in our constant great hurry, often jar with the landscape. The Natives are in accordance with it, and when the tall, slim, dark, and dark-eyed people travel – always one by one, so that even the great native veins of traffic are narrow footpaths – or work the soil, or herd the cattle, or hold their big dances, or tell you a tale, it is Africa wandering, dancing, and entertaining you. In the highlands you remember the poet's words, 'Noble found I, ever the native and insipid the immigrant'.

Her picture was that of an East Africa of the 1920s, from her 6,000 acre farm in the Ngong Hills, where her natives were squatters. Our sense of Africa, some thirty years later, seemed far removed from this world of the White Highlands.

Karamoja occupied a vast area of north-eastern Uganda, stretching from the Sudan in the north and bordering Kenya almost all the way to Lake Victoria. Most of the region was flat semi-desert with little rainfall, but a long line of high mountains formed the eastern frontier: these attracted the little rain that fell and were green above the arid plain. Entry to the territory was prohibited, except by special pass. The main reason for this was that the authorities wanted to impose order where the local population made their own laws, according to their own needs. To the Karamojong people, the cattle herds represented wealth as well as being their main livelihood, and this, combined with the problem of perennial droughts, led to a culture of cattle-raiding across boundaries of other groups. Violence was always possible in these encounters and the Karamojong men saw themselves as warriors.

Our passes were issued without any fuss: visitors to the region were few, and white people, not connected to government, were not seen as a threat. We set off with a little trepidation. This was to be the longest safari we would undertake in our tiny Fiat. In addition, Eoin was with us: he was now one year old and quite active. The car had developed a reputation for using more water than petrol and both liquids would be scarce where we were heading. The main problem was the water pump, which had a tendency to seize and require taking apart for cleaning. I had become reasonably adept at this operation but if it happened far out in the bush, could I cope? The engine in the Fiat was in the rear and the front boot was too shallow for large containers. We settled for a five-gallon tin of water, which was tied on the rear seat, and hoped we could keep topping up with petrol whenever we came to a garage. A small canvas sack of drinking water was fixed to the front grille: the traditional cooling method.

The first stage out of Kampala was easy: the road to Jinja, the source of the Nile, was the longest stretch of tarmac in Uganda. We left the lush forests that surrounded Lake Victoria, the road turned north and the surface deteriorated rapidly. For a while we thought that our little car would fall apart from

GATEWAY TO KARAMOJA

the constant pounding over the corrugations and endless
potholes. It was exhausting, concentrating on keeping clear of
deep side channels, but sharing the driving helped and it felt
less claustrophobic when the open savannah widened our
horizon.

Some time after leaving the last large town, Mbale, I could
feel the car struggling. I knew the signs: an overheating engine
and a drying radiator. The road was empty. We had seen no
other traffic for ages and a deserted countryside all around us.
We managed to halt under the dappled shade of a clump of
acacia trees: there was no option but to let the engine cool
down.

We opened the car doors to encourage a breeze and sit out the wait, while Eoin played in the warm sand under the trees. Three figures suddenly appeared – two youths, one with a bicycle, and a little girl. This always seemed to happen: when the landscape looked empty, someone would pop up from behind a bush or materialize from nowhere: was a kind of bush telegraph operating? We had a lively chat for a while before they moved off. I tried to open the radiator cap and nearly got scalded. After about an hour it felt safe to refill the radiator and then began to dismantle the water pump and clean out the red murram dust that had choked it. I was now an expert at this operation and soon had it reassembled. A moment of tension before the key was turned: would the engine start? Careful not to flood the carburettor, easy on the accelerator and we were off, reassured by the smooth, sewing machine-like hum of the motor.

It was now mid-afternoon and we were passing close to the edge of Lake Salisbury. This was part of a vast system of interlocking lakes and wetlands where the Nile, pouring over the falls at Jinja, spread out over the plains. We paused at this scene of tranquil beauty. The placid waters reflected the blue sky and the shoreline was fringed with a carpet of white and mauve water lilies. An astonishing coral tree, leafless but covered with masses of pink blossoms, completed the picture; it was like a painting by Monet. When we drove into the small town of Soroti, there were still 70 miles to travel before the border with Karamoja. Although there was still plenty of daylight left, we agreed that a halt for us, and the car, would be restorative. We arranged to spend the night at the Government Rest House where we were the only guests. We sat out

SOROTI ROCK

on the shady veranda with cold drinks and contemplated this
sleepy place, which seemed like a ghost town, where nothing
stirred and few cars were parked on the wide street.

For some time I had been fascinated by a remarkable
feature just outside the last houses: a huge dome-shaped rock
standing straight up from the flat landscape. I strolled over a
sea of yellow dry grass to the foot of the monolith and
immediately had to climb to the top. An easy scramble
brought me on to the rounded bare summit and a spectacular panorama in every direction. There was a bird's eye view
of the little town: revealed as laid out in a grid pattern with a
wide boulevard in the centre. The two-storied buildings were
overwhelmingly white and, together with the square geom-
etry of the tiny settlement, made a stark presence in the wide
and lonely plain. Dark cloud shadows marched over the flat
lands to the north-east where the faint outlines of mountains

were just visible. These were more than 100 miles away and our objective for the next day.

When we left the police post at Lothaa and crossed the invisible line of the border of Karamoja, the landscape seemed to change, although the wide plain still seemed endless and the distant mountains no nearer. Spindly thorn trees shone silvery in the midday sun and the gracefully rounded green tops of the acacias belied the arid ground, where it looked as if no rain had fallen for a long time.

The road ended at Moroto, a small scattering of blockwork bungalows, each roofed with corrugated iron sheets. The tiny settlement was tucked in close to the foot of the huge bulk of Mount Moroto, over 10,000 feet high, and towering some 6,000 feet above the town. We drove across the beaten red earth to the rest camp and were astonished to be met by a pair of ostriches. They scampered past us, twisting their heads, seemingly at right angles, and giving us supercilious looks. Small groups of Karamojong stood around, watching us silently. The men were tall, thin and sharp-featured, naked except for short black cloaks fixed at the neck, and every warrior carried a spear. The few women we saw stayed well in the background and each was carrying a bundle.

The company that evening in the rest camp was mixed: a couple of government officials, a pair of tourists like ourselves, and an interesting young man who seemed very knowledgeable about the Karamojong and their customs. Robert, an anthropologist, had been living in the territory for more than a year, immersing himself in the culture. He told us that he had a camp some miles to the north and invited us to come and spend the next day with him. We were delighted. It seemed a great opportunity to learn something more credible about this strange place: up to now our education had been in the form of tales from the expatriate community in Kampala, never the most reliable source.

There was no road marked on the map to Robert's camp but from his directions, we followed a faint trail that wound between trees: tire-marks eventually led us on a gentle rise to a flat tableland, with widening views over the plains. The camp was in a shallow sandy depression, half-ringed with acacias and facing a tremendous prospect of Mount Moroto. The tent was pitched under the shade of the trees, but it was a tent like no other we had ever seen. It was low-slung but spread out over a huge area; it was wide open in front, flaps tied up along with mosquito netting. The encampments of Bedouins in the Sahara came to mind. Canvas screens divided the interior into several rooms, the largest being the living area and workspace. Comfortable deckchairs and loungers made it highly appealing. We could live here, we both thought.

An enthusiastic Robert gave us a tour of his domain: his generator; Tilley lamps; camp bed – covered with another fine mosquito net – typewriter; stacks of books and papers and finally his lavatory, 50 yards out in the bush. This consisted of a deep hole dug in the ground and covered by a toilet seat perched on flat stones. The contraption was surrounded by a canvas screen and, in the parlance of East African settlers, was known as a 'thunder box'. He took us for a short walk behind the camp where, to our amazement, we spotted a small herd of camels. These were wild, he explained, probably descended from the pack animals that accompanied early expeditions from the Sudan to find the source of the Nile. Arab slavers also used camels on their forays from the coast to the interior.

Back at the camp, we relaxed in the shade of the tent and Robert told us about the Karamojong, their non-conforming life and ways of dealing with strangers. We gathered that one of his most important studies was of their language, about which little was known. The first surveyors and mapmakers had trouble fixing names for prominent hills and other land features when they enquired from the locals. The conversations, Robert said, often went like this: 'What do you call this hill?' from the surveyor, pointing. 'Lokitok', from the local: duly noted by the official. 'And this', pointing to another eminence. 'Lokitoktok', being the reply. Translated, the names supplied by the Karamojong were, 'heap of shit' and 'another heap of shit'.

The bravery of these people was legendary. One of the ways that a young man could prove himself as a warrior was on a lion hunt. An ever-tightening, spear-wielding circle would surround a lone animal, the lion would charge and the man in the way would have to kill it or be killed. It was a sort of Russian roulette. Reinforcing this story, Robert told us of an incident in the territory where the District Commissioner called the elders of a certain village to a meeting. He admonished them regarding a recent cattle raid and warned that it must not be repeated. The next morning the severed head of a lion was left on the doorstep of his office.

The elders of the tribe made the rules and all decisions were taken at regular meetings. Robert, in the early stages of his sojourn, decided to attend one of these meetings. He arrived and sat down in the circle of elders, who at first ignored him but nobody spoke until a senior member of the tribe said that he should not be there. 'Why not?' said Robert. There was a long pause and then he was told that he was not old enough and that only men over thirty could attend. Robert lied and said that he was over thirty and continued sitting in the circle. Silence prevailed, again for a long time until eventually his presence was accepted and the meeting went on.

The warrior status seemed sufficient for the Karamojong men. They did no work, except go on occasional cattle raids. Apart from this activity, according to Robert, their main occupation was doing their hair. Extraordinarily elaborate hair constructions were made with red mud and these were worn with great pride. At this stage we had been enjoying several bottles of beer from his little camp fridge. Our friend then told us of an adventure he had had with the local group, when he was inveigling himself into their confidence. He was invited to join a night-time hunt of wild dogs: the preliminary being a beer-drinking session in one of the shelters. He decided to strip naked before he sat down in the circle of warriors where gourds of home brew were passed around. He had learned quite a bit of the language by this time and at one stage, when everybody was quite drunk, he admired the hair do of the warrior nearest him. 'You are my friend', the man cried out. 'I will give it to you.' He promptly produced a knife and sliced off the concoction of mud and hair and presented it to Robert. Suddenly appalled at what he had done, the warrior broke down in tears and our friend feared for his life. Fortunately the hunt began soon after. Robert was handed a spear, but he said that they were all too drunk to do more than prance around in the dark.

Before we left, Robert produced a Karamojong spear, which, he said, had been confiscated by the District Commissioner from a warrior who was carrying two. One was allowed for defence but carrying two was considered to demonstrate aggression. It was a beautiful object, slender and shapely. Made in three sections, the centre, the holding part, was hardened wood, while the top metal piece was finished with a wickedly sharp leaf-shaped blade. The end section was metal with a delicately tapered pointed tip. We could not fit it into the car, but eventually managed to dismantle it by heating the joins and softening the tar that glued together the sections. Thanking our host, we drove off, hoping the police would not search our car. That evening the mountain was dark-etched against a blazing starlit sky and no breeze stirred the silence.

I had planned to try climbing Mount Moroto but reaching the main summit, I had been told, involved a two-day trek. This meant hiring porters, from a usually reluctant local population, to carry water and camping gear. There was a subsidiary peak, Imagit, that was just over 9,000 feet and it looked to be a feasible one-day climb. An enticing-looking ridge pointed a way up from the flat plain. The summit was just visible from the settlement but the final sections were blocked from view by a high rocky shoulder. I was confident that a way could be found around this and, after that, a route to the top might be revealed.

I started just after dawn, alone, and from the end of the red dusty track took a line that, I hoped, would bring me on to the ridge. It quickly became hot and oppressive among the thickly clustered trees and bushes. It was difficult to plot a straight course and in the dryness, fallen dead branches crackled underfoot. The trees eventually thinned out and the route was clear ahead. Nearly three hours of climbing in draining heat brought me to the base of the rocky shoulder. It was time for a rest. I could now see down into the deep gorge that separated the two ridges leading to the summit. Where the mouth of the gorge widened, a sea of thick forest spilled out to end at the foot of the mountain and the level plain. A large clearing was visible in the carpet of trees: a Karamojong *boma*, a circular enclosure fenced with thorns, with a huddle of huts in the centre. The cattle were rounded up at night and herded into the refuge to protect them from predators. It occurred to me that these predators were likely to be lions and leopards, and it was hard to push this thought aside. The experts said that, with the possible exception of buffalo, most wild creatures would avoid contact with humans. This aphorism was all very well in the comfort of company, but out alone in the bush I felt a flutter of unease.

The feeling stayed with me as I edged around the steep shoulder to find a way past. Small trees ringed the base of the rocks and as I passed under the canopy I heard a rustle above. I was petrified and froze. Could it be a leopard? Impossible to see in the dappled sunlight and shade. I forced myself to move slowly away and did not relax until I was well out on the open ground. A sharp strenuous pull up a dusty gully led out to another gently sloping ridge and a delicious cool breeze.

Three antelope bounded off over the crest. The ridge swooped up ahead, yellow-green, deep grass to the graceful summit. I was now only 6,000 feet up, with over 3,000 still to go. I plunged along the high lonely uplands, feeling an overwhelming sense of isolation with the immensity of the great plain rising below. I went fast – at a punishing pace almost – driven by a queer sense of urgency.

I remembered the first time I had climbed alone. I was about eleven and it was also my first mountain, albeit only the hill behind the family home. Out on the windswept, heathery moor and near the top I heard a harsh cry 'go bak – go bak – go bak.' It was a grouse calling but I could still recall the sudden fright. The same feeling gripped me now. A sharp steep cliff, with spiky aloes at the base, barred the ridge. I scrambled up this breathlessly and suddenly came out on the rim of the gorge. Waving grass in a wide sweep led to the summit cone. It was midday.

A stupendous panorama unfolded, such as I had never seen. Nearby, across a wide ravine, was the main summit of Mount Moroto – a tawny huge shape with a polka dot pattern of bushes reaching up to a sharply etched dark pinnacle. To the west the plain of central Karamoja opened up to a high horizon with the blue-grey peaks of Napak and Akisim, ghostly shapes in the haze. To the north, the low yellow and ochre hills heaped one upon the other all the way to the Sudan border, beyond which were two thousand miles of desert. To the east, a strange golden light suffused the air, and heat haze filtered out the forms of hills in the Kenya Northern Frontier country to Lake Rudolph and the Ethiopian highlands. Southwards, the great plain stretched a hundred

MOUNT MOROTO

miles to the savage crags of Kadam, and the monstrous, cloudy bulk of Mount Elgon lay like a great whale along the southern horizon.

I had the first drink of water since leaving the road head and shivered in sudden awareness of the cold breeze. I started down, deciding to use another ridge and thus complete a circuit of the gorge. No maps of the mountain existed, so entering here had a flavour of true exploration. Some, with justification, frowned upon solo climbing but great rewards were also possible. The experience of high adventure was intense; there was potency in the overcoming of a challenge and, above all, encounters with the natural world are deeper when one is alone.

When I reached the far end of the gorge, a steep slope halted me. Staring down, I could see that a network of danger-ous-looking crags traced across the slope as far as I could see. There was no way around and trying to find a way down, alone, was too risky. I was tired now and it was getting hot again, away from the cooling heights. Opening my water bottle for a drink, I managed to let it fall over and every drop was spilt. This was serious. It was still a long way down and I could not see an easy route. I then made a very bad decision: a classic bad decision. It was to go straight down to the gorge and then follow the watercourse to the open valley. The golden rule is: never follow a watercourse in the mountains since it was almost always unpredictable and frequently precipitous. I knew the rule but the way seemed shorter and there was the possibility of finding water in pools that had not dried.

A track of sorts lured me on down in the direction of the gorge but it soon began to follow a contouring line and was obviously an animal trail. Worse still, it began to lead me farther up the wall of the gorge in the opposite direction to the one I wanted. The track faded and I found myself floundering in a sea of long yellow grass interlaced with brambles. This was the time to stop and make a decision: do I go on or retrace my steps back to the ridge and find an alternative path? The thought of going back up the steep slope, when my legs were now so tired, made me stick to my original idea of getting down to the watercourse.

The heat was now like a hammer on my head. A vertical sun beat straight into the enclosed space of the ravine and all the greenery reflected a silvery glare. My contour line eventually led me to the floor of the gorge, but much higher up than I had hoped. The watercourse was dry. The water-polished rocky bed was hot to the touch and there was no vestige of a lingering pool. I struggled down the bed of the river for a short way, watching out for any remaining water in shady corners, but was stopped by a wall of brambles and thorns, savagely entangled in a choking mass. I scrambled up the right flank of the gorge to avoid the obstacle until more thorn thickets barred my passage. The only way was to crawl under the thick bushes. This worked for a while and I made some slow progress, in a parallel line to the watercourse, until I was halted by a steep cliff.

Back down to the riverbed: still no water, and up the far side to repeat the battle endlessly until I was exhausted. I had travelled barely two hundred yards. A tiny clearing around a cedar tree offered some blessed shade and I lay down and fell asleep. I awoke to feel the huge hot arc of sun and sky overhead and saw the dappled patches of shade dancing in a haze.

I was desperate now. My tongue felt swollen with thirst and my whole body was becoming dehydrated. I remember falling head first down a 15-foot slab of rock and being hardly able to crawl out of the thorn bushes that broke my fall. My shirt and shorts were torn and shredded and I was covered in cuts and scratches. There was a gleam of water ahead. I rushed towards it, mad with thirst, to find a viscous green shallow pool, choked with slimy weeds. This was a stagnant residue of the last rains that must have roared down, tearing and flattening foliage and racing out over the valley floor and then out into the dusty plain to die away in the arid emptiness. The very thought worsened my thirst. I tried to drink but but had to spit out the vile-tasting stuff. Half-delirious, I went on and on, crawling more often than walking: now thinking that I could die. The sun was well down in the sky when I sensed that the thorn bushes were less dense. I was out of the gorge!

The wide valley opened out before me with innumerable tracks crossing and recrossing, winding in and out of densely packed trees. I sat down to rest and must have dozed for a little but quickly became aware of being watched. I turned my head and saw a naked, dusty black figure standing in the shade looking at me: a young Karamojong warrior. He had a red feather stuck into his stiff clay-caulked hair and the two spears he was holding were taller than he was. He did not move but continued to stand there silently with an expressionless stare. I tried to speak but could only croak in Swahili and ask if there was water nearby. After a long scrutiny he moved off, but turned and made a small gesture as if to follow him. He loped down a gently sloping trail and I staggered after him, trying with great difficulty to keep up. He quickly disappeared from sight in the maze of trees and I was sure that I had lost the faint trail I was following. The going was easier now and I continued in a general downhill direction for about a mile when there he was again, standing as if waiting for me. There was no doubt that he knew where I was all the time. He moved off, slowly this time, and after a few minutes pointed to a shady bank and a deep hole where clouds of flies wheeled and buzzed. I drank and drank from this unsavoury-looking place and water never tasted sweeter.

The youth stayed with me as the trail widened into a definite well-beaten track through taller trees. Turning a

corner, we came into a large clearing where a party of
Karamojong were squatting in a circle. My companion joined
them and I tried to explain, in Swahili and by pointing, where
I had been. They didn't seem particularly interested, so, after
I said *kwa heri* – goodbye – I went on down the track.

Dogs yelped at me from a *boma* nearby and, as the path
became broader, I came out to the dirt road from where I had
started in the early morning. A small dark pool under a rock
overhang had been formed by seepage from mossy bogs. I
stripped off my torn shirt and shorts and slipped into the
velvet smooth water. I lay there a long time as the blue of the
sky changed to ultramarine and, when insects began to rise
and dart, I dressed and walked out of the forest. The loud
hum of cicadas filled the night and somewhere in the darkness
of the plain a solitary drum began to beat.

The map that we had of Karamoja was rudimentary: its main
purpose seemed to delineate administrative boundaries and
the links between them. It was large-scale and detail was
scanty, leaving huge areas between roads as empty spaces. The
territory appeared as a vast plain bounded by continuous
mountains on the eastern frontier. The floor of the plain
mapped an intricate lacework of thin blue lines, like veins, as
if a region of waterways existed, where fertile land could be
expected. The reality was that the whole area was semi-desert
and all these watercourses could stay dry for years. Intrigu-
ingly, many of the streamlines and even tributaries had names,
showing how important even sporadic water flows or residual
ponds were to pastoral tribes in arid places. We hoped they
would all stay dry for our journey back.

This map was a challenge for the planning of our return route. Those empty spaces were a siren call to discovery: the enormous skies and spreading open landscapes of Karamoja were an exciting tonic after the claustrophobic jungles around Kampala. The roads, though, were now our main concern. The thick red line on the map was described as 1st Class, the thin red line as 2nd Class, and the 3rd Class was shown as a dotted red line. The thin dotted black lines were described as 'Suitable for foot traffic only.'

On another bright morning with a perfect day promised, it was easy to feel emboldened, after our successful journey to this wild place. Why not try a different way back and explore some of those empty spaces on the map? The most attractive prospect was to travel down the eastern side, close to the mountains. The problem was that only one thin red line led this way and after about 50 miles it turned into Kenya and the Rift Valley. A dotted red line continued south for another 30 miles before it too turned east for the Kenya frontier, leaving a gap of some 30 miles across an empty space. Close scrutiny of the map showed a faint dotted black track that joined a minor road, which then connected to the main artery for Kampala. This ought not to be a problem for our car, we thought, having easily negotiated the almost trackless terrain to Robert's camp. The designation 'suitable for foot traffic only' we blithely ignored.

Before leaving, Nuala spoke of her day at the Rest Camp while I was on the mountain. She went out in the cool of the morning carrying Eoin, African fashion, across one hip, to walk to a grove of mimosa and acacia trees. The pair of ostriches was still wandering around, obviously semi-domesticated and attached to the District Commissioner's headquarters. Our little boy played in the sand under the trees until the heat of the day drove them back indoors. Nuala said that she was sitting reading while Eoin was playing on the floor: suddenly looking up, she saw a tall, black, naked figure silhouetted in the open doorway against the bright sunlight. A Karamojong warrior stood there; spear in hand, scrap of cloth pinned at his neck. Then, without a word, he moved off along the veranda. Nuala, initially startled, was then curious and went out through the door to see what was happening. The man had parked his spear against the wall and was busy opening a bundle from which he produced a lump of putty. He then squatted down and began to mould strips of this along the frames of the window where sections were missing. This activity seemed to give the lie to the stories Robert and others told us that Karamojong males did no work, leaving all such demeaning business to the women. Perhaps working for the government did not threaten their warrior status.

I filled the Fiat's tank from the single petrol pump in Moroto, topped up the water tin and we were ready to start the journey back. A few miles outside the town we turned due south on the first leg of our new return route. It was, however, with some little trepidation that we realized we were heading into unknown territory. It was 50 miles to Nabilatuk – the last settlement before we attempted to cross the empty spaces to some kind of civilization, on the far side of the border of Karamoja. We crossed the first of the innumerable watercourses marked on the map and, after negotiating a half-dozen or so, relaxed in the knowledge that each was bone dry. Driving on this second-class road was much easier than on the earlier main roads: there was little or no traffic, with the result that the shuddering corrugations of the red murram surface were few.

Trailing a long plume of dust, we made steady progress across the flats: wide open spaces, dotted with graceful acacias and a huge bowl of clear sky overhead. It was an exhilarating transit: our confidence grew with each mile covered. The main hazard was soft sand. Swathes of this sometimes drifted across the road and its creamy, almost liquid, texture could send us swirling off the track. We settled into a rhythm: slow down, keep a straight line and watch for the next blinding white patch up ahead. After a couple of hours we stopped for a rest and to let the engine cool. There was a gap in the hills to the east and when we walked up to a little knoll there was a superb view of the barren wastelands out to the Kenya Rift Valley. Tumbled masses of red-ochre uplands were progressively lost in a purple haze and the most distant forms danced, as undulating mirages, along the horizon.

At the tiny settlement of Nabilatuk it was time for a decision. Do we turn west here and take a short cut back to the main road of our outward journey – the safe option – or do we go on? The remote landscape beckoned: so far, our progress had been nearly effortless and it was still early in the day. We went on. The third-class road was now a mere track, wandering over the arid lands and winding past rocky knolls or thorny hillocks.

Kadam mountain now loomed ahead. From a distance of twenty miles it appeared as a long blue massif that gradually split, as we drove nearer, into two separate peaks. Our track wound closer to the foot of the mountain that rose to over 10,000 feet: the lushly green forests on the early slopes were a stark contrast to the dry plain. We had heard that the Kadama and Tepeth people inhabited the forests around the mountain. They were said to be a primitive and easy-going clan, who had, in the past, been driven into the mountain areas by the warlike Karamojong.

We followed along the western flank of the mountain to where the road turned east towards the Kenya frontier. It was somewhere here that we hoped to find the lesser track that would take us back to Mbale and the main road home. We drove along slowly, watching out for any sign of a track turning off to the south. For about ten miles along the forest edge there was not the slightest trace of a possible passage. Our anxiety now was: does this way actually exist or will we have to abandon the venture and take the long way back? Just as the edge of the forest made a sharp turn east there it was: a narrow sandy trail leading in the direction we wanted. We stopped and walked along it for a few yards to look for signs of previous use and quickly found some faint traces of tyre-marks. Another car had been along here but when? It hadn't rained for months, but it was an encouraging sign.

Thirty miles of empty space now faced us: there were no habitations and no guarantee that the track did lead to civilization, but there was still six hours of daylight left so we set off with confidence. After a couple of miles we stopped close to some shady trees. We needed a good rest and it was imperative to allow the radiator to cool before setting out on the last leg into the unknown. The three of us must have dozed off for when we awoke we were astonished to look out at a herd of at least a dozen giraffes standing near and staring down at the car. It was a strange and enchanting spectacle:

the reticulated pattern on hides and long necks merged with the dappled shade of the acacias. The heads of the animals reached as high as the rounded canopies of leaves and each pair of huge eyes gazed fixedly at us. I slowly reached for my camera and carefully lowered my window, just managing to take a few shots before the enormous creatures leaped up and galloped away. They halted after a couple of hundred yards and, obviously curious, looked back at the car. I started the engine and slowly circled out into the bush to get nearer to the herd. As soon as we moved, they ran off and I speeded up to chase them, managing to get a few more pictures before they disappeared. We had now left the trail, however, and it took a little while, and some anxious moments, before we picked it up again.

It was necessary to wait again for the radiator to cool and as soon as it was safe to unscrew the lid, I topped up with our spare water and we were on our way once more. For some time, we had become aware that many of the latter watercourses had been filled with deeper sand requiring an increasing effort to push through. We were now approaching what was, by far, the biggest blue line shown on the map – the Greek River, or Siti as it was described. We hoped this would be dry, it being fed by both Kadam and the much larger Mount Elgon.

Suddenly it was there before us: a wide expanse of blinding white sand, at least two hundred yards across but, thankfully, completely dry. We started to cross, in the lowest gear, but after less than thirty yards, churned to a halt: all four wheels were buried to the hubs in the powdery stuff. We were miles from any village; the next vehicle on this road might not appear for weeks; the sun was scorching hot and we were stuck fast. We stood, looking at our stranded car, and eventually agreed that it could be worse – it could be raining!

There was no hint of cloud on those mountains, now faintly hazy in the heat of the day but this might not last. We had to try to get free. There were two large tin plates in our kit for safari food stops and we each used one of these to scoop a straight channel out from the front wheels. We did the same for the rear wheels until all four were clear. It was time to attempt to move. I got ready to push from the rear while Nuala started the engine, engaged low gear and gently let out the clutch. At the right moment I started to push and the car moved, inch by inch until, with a jolt, it shot forward for another 50 yards or so until it got stuck again. We repeated the exercise several more times until the tyres finally bit into hard ground and we rolled over onto the far bank.

Eoin slept through all this, but we were exhausted from the heat and the effort. We could congratulate ourselves, however, that our little Fiat could be coaxed across such a formidable obstacle. There was still a long way to go and we wondered if we had now burnt our bridges and reached the dreaded 'point of no return'. It was futile to think about the difficulty of retreat: we had to go on. Mile after mile the level plain stretched ahead: the horizon a shivering line in the afternoon heat. The track, though faint, was still possible to follow, even when we had to swerve off the route to avoid sand-filled dips and fallen dead trees. Ahead of us the huge bulk of Mount Elgon began to emerge from the misty haze until, at last, it was clear and sharply defined to the east of our route. At least we were heading in the right direction.

Far away across the flat landscape, and to our left, I saw a long trailing cloud of red dust and it appeared to be moving: another vehicle, and it was on a road. We had crossed the empty space! All that was necessary now was to point the car at that dusty cloud until the lifeline of the red murram corrugations led us back to civilization.

CHAPTER 9

DARK DAYS

Starting into our third year in Uganda I think that we both felt
the beginning of a sense of disenchantment.

W E W E R E E A C H H A P P Y in our work; our baby
son was thriving; pineapples, mangos, bananas
and pawpaws constantly filled our fruit basket; we
had explored widely, had many friends and every single,
solitary day the sun shone from that blue, blue sky. So what
was wrong? Why this vague feeling of discontent? It may have
been because of the fact of those endless sunny days and,
above all, that there were no seasons. It was difficult to fix
with any surety when a certain event had taken place. A
particular month had no significance; April could easily be
August or November, so far as the zenith of the sun at noon
was concerned. At least December was Christmas, but there
was no solstice, which to me had always held huge meaning.

It was still, of course, a pleasure to walk out in the calm
of the African morning, to listen to the dawn chorus of exotic
birds and, above all, to feel the warm sun on bodies free of
heavy clothes. On the way to work each morning, the flagrant
brilliance of the scarlet hibiscus and the carmine red and
purple bougainvillea could lift the spirits but the pervasive,

deep green of plantain and forest began to dull the senses. I remembered the infinite shades of green back home in the waving grasses of a June meadow: olive, bronze, sage, viridian, malachite. Here in the centre of Africa the deciduous trees never shed their leaves at the same time. An individual specimen would each follow its own rhythm and in the forest a single leafless tree would stand starkly against the dense foliage of its fellows.

It was this rhythm of the seasons in our own selves that was missing on the Equator. Drowsily sitting by the Silver

GREEN JUNGLE, KAMPALA

Springs swimming pool, I had little nostalgia for those dark December mornings, when cold rain dripped from the bare branches in that far north. But spring inevitably followed with the smell of wild garlic in the woods and the young shoots on the larches and beeches. Then the steady progression of other delights of nature: wild roses and perfumed woodbine tangled in the hedges; the blaze of yellow furze; meadowsweet and purple loosestrife on roadside verges and then the slow march to autumn fruits and inexorable decay. The whole cycle of renewal must begin again; birth and rebirth; fresh anticipation for every new year.

I missed the watercolour tones of Ireland the most; opalescent grey washes of skies streaked with pale blue and the melting hues of bogland browns and umbers. Here, the unrelieved monotone of the terracotta red earth impoverished the landscape's palette of colours and I was growing tired of it. I had also lived most of my life in sight of the sea and now, a thousand miles in the interior, I wanted to view the ever-changing ocean and smell and hear the sound of crashing waves.

In addition to all these increasingly frequent bouts of nostalgia and homesickness, there was an unsettling feeling in the transient nature of our abode in Africa. The small white population was constantly shifting and changing, with friends departing on long leave or for good. Jean and Philip had left for Nairobi – Philip's firm had moved him to a new road contract in Kenya. The hierarchy of colour and race made it difficult to cross the boundaries. Even our home on Mbuya was seeing change. For our first two years the little community felt snug and secure in the forest clearing. We could walk to the swimming pool along single tracks through the elephant grass and tall trees, past *shambas* where little African children played – Eoin sometimes joined them – but now this was ending. Bulldozers had moved in, felling trees and clearing the bush for a large scheme of government housing.

Suddenly, in these changing times our whole world was turned upside down. Nuala went into hospital in the May of that year for the birth of our second child. Everything seemed normal and Nuala came home after a couple of days, but the newborn baby boy was kept in – for further checks, we were told. When we called back next day we were told that there was a problem and that the doctor would come and talk to us. It was a worrying wait in that grimly antiseptic place and we sat in silence, each with our own thoughts. We must have waited for almost an hour, although in our state of apprehensiveness it seemed far longer, when a middle-aged man appeared. He told us bluntly that our baby had a serious heart problem and that the hospital could do little to alleviate his condition. He then delivered a devastating opinion: the baby's chances of survival were poor; the only possibility of treatment was to take him to London and to the Great Ormond Street Hospital for Children where they had top-class facilities. In his opinion, however, he did not think that he would survive much beyond the age of ten even if treated in London. He told us that the baby could not be moved for some time, but that we should go home and think about what we were going to do.

We went away from the building, shaken and demoralized, but much worse was the sense of hopelessness. We were in Africa, far away from family. How could we uproot again and make another new life so soon after the old one had been left behind? My mind was in a turmoil of emotions: the tiny morsel fighting for his life; could we get enough money to afford the trip to London; would I be able to get another job? It was the worst day of our lives.

We visited our baby son every day for over a week, but there was no change. He was baptized and we named him Niall. On the eleventh day after his birth Nuala and I made our usual morning visit. When we arrived outside the nurses' station, we noticed that the window to the baby care unit was wide open and we had a premonition that something had changed. The nurse appeared and told us that Niall had died from a heart attack during the night. The hospital asked our permission to carry out an autopsy and, too overcome to reason otherwise, we agreed.

It was a few days before we were told the results of the autopsy: the baby was born, we were informed, with a highly unusual heart condition which made it difficult for him to breathe properly. It was a consolation, albeit a small one, to be told that his chances of survival were never great. Nothing was written down and we were too dejected to ask any questions. We just walked away.

We had passed the cemetery on the Jinga road every morning on the way to work, never aware that one day it would become a place that would be permanently fixed in our lives. One of the roadside workshops made a little coffin and had it painted white. The funeral was a small affair: just our friends and especially Walter, who gave us stalwart support. I brought the tiny casket on the rear seat of the car and, after we had made a procession of sorts, I carried it in my arms to near the top of the cemetery where a grave had already been prepared. After the diminutive coffin was laid to rest, we waited until the filling in was complete and one of our friends laid a single bloom of red hibiscus on the mound. We turned to leave and walked down the path under the shade of the gentle mimosa and acacias in utter sadness.

Nothing seemed ever the same after Niall's death. Unsettled seemed to be the word that described our circumstance but could also be applied to the territory. *Uhuru*, freedom, or officially, Independence, was promised in just two years for Uganda. An architectural competition had been held for the new Parliament building for an independent Uganda. The prize been won by the British firm of architects, Peatfield and Bogdener, and the complex was now being built on the hill overlooking our office. There was, however, growing unrest, though nobody seemed to agree on the main reasons for this.

Truckloads of youths took to driving through the city shouting slogans and jeering at Europeans. The tone, however, was more good-humoured than hostile and, in the usual African manner, there was a great deal of laughter. Nevertheless the authorities reacted strongly and, in a typical colonial response, sent in the military. The rhythmic sound of tramping boots brought us out of the office one morning to see a solid file of soldiers, shouldering rifles with bayonets fixed, marching up Grant Street. It was the fourth battalion of the King's African Rifles, the Uganda section of the much larger regiment, based mainly in Kenya. Two white officers, in khaki shorts and tunics, strode at the front of the column of black troops, each in a uniform of a dark jersey, topped with a red fez: the archetypical symbol of Empire.

There had been argument and dispute in the newspapers about the 'problem of the lost counties'. This, to us, had a familiar ring since in Ireland the partition of the island in 1922 had led to the rise of the same catch phrase. However, in Uganda we learned that the dispute had a far older history, reaching back to Speke and Baker's sojourn with King Kamrasi of Bunyoro and even earlier. The protectorate of Uganda was, before the arrival of the British, a jumble of separate kingdoms, many of which were at war with each other. Buganda had welcomed the British at the close of the nineteenth century and had acquired seven counties, formerly part of Bunyoro. The story of the dispute over the 'lost counties' between Bunyoro and Buganda was testimony to this bitter antagonism and often erupted in the Legislative Council. With independence only a few years away, animosities between the districts or ancient kingdoms of the territory were a portent of troubled times.

When the monthly magazine *Drum* was launched in South Africa in the early 1950s, it was hugely welcomed by a black African population that was becoming more urbanized and more impatient with white minority rule. A white businessman started the publication and the first editors were also white, but it was targeted almost exclusively at black readers. *Drum* appeared on the newstands of Kampala very quickly after its launch and its lively layout, creative photography and investigative articles by black journalists appealed equally to Africans in Uganda, urgent for change.

This unsettling atmosphere began to affect the practice. The partners took to holding meetings most days, behind closed doors, which in normal times were always open. Inglis was even more taciturn than usual, while McGuinness had lost some of his sparkle and geniality. The Sikhs were often whispering together and Chana was spending less time looking out of the window. The only person I could confide in was Walter, and we arranged to join colleagues from an associated quantity surveyors' firm for a lunch at the City Bar to try to find out if anyone knew what was happening. The gathering could only recount rumours; new commissions were generally slowing; firms were considering relocating to South Africa or even Southern Rhodesia where white rule was still paramount. The only solid consensus was that redundancies were to be expected.

Insecurity was in the nature of the world of architectural practice: periods of feast and famine alternated, where commissions for new work were concerned. This, however, was puzzling to me since the practice appeared to have plenty of work and everybody was busy. I had several big projects on my drawing board: an office block with shops at ground level and the largest project yet won by the firm – a multi-storey headquarters for the Bank of India. At lunchtime one day I was still in the drawing office after everyone else had left: I was engrossed in finishing a perspective rendering of the bank. On my way out to return some files to the anti-room, I overheard a snatch of conversation from the office of one of the partners: the door had been left ajar because they obviously thought that everyone had left. The tail end of a sentence from the senior partner went, 'for the present anyway we'll have to keep Ryder, at least to finish the supervision of the remaining jobs.'

I left as silently as I could, thinking this was the beginning of the end. I told Nuala later that day what I had overheard and that the speculation was over and we must make plans for our future. In our early months in Africa we were hugely optimistic and daily living was carefree: a long-term life based in Uganda could be easily embraced. Becoming parents had changed our vision: schools, for instance, were racially segregated; European older children were invariably sent for boarding to schools overseas. Our baby's death further disillusioned us about settling for a permanent stay in Africa. We wanted to go home.

In the weeks that followed nothing was said at work, but there was an increasing feeling that the changing times were leading to an ending of certainties. Over sundowners one evening in the City Bar a colleague from an associated firm caustically remarked, 'rats and sinking ships are on the menu today'. I told Walter about my overheard remark but he said that he was also thinking of leaving once his three-year contract had ended.

Nuala and I made up our minds: we would leave Africa for good and go home. My contract still had about five months to run, but there were several immediate decisions we would have to make before our departure. The first problem was the matter of our possessions. We had to choose whether to travel back home by air or by sea.

We loved our little car and wanted to keep it, so that decision was easy: it would travel back with us – on board ship. The problem with our other possessions was more difficult: as well as deciding what to take and what to leave, there was the need to have crates packed well in advance of our departure. It would mean leaving our house and finding furnished accommodation for a short while. This could be expensive and we had to save money for an uncertain future back in Ireland.

Nuala sugested a simple answer: our close friends, Jean and Philip, had offered to have us stay with them in Nairobi any time we wished. If she and Eoin went there and if I could find somewhere to stay, while working out the remainder of my contract, we could leave our house on Mbuya, sell or pack all our belongings and in the process save some money. Walter said that I could rent a room in the Bachelors' Quarters at a low rent, so the way was clear to make the move. Nuala and Eoin would travel by train to Nairobi while I would join them later, driving from Kampala. We would all then travel on to Mombasa to board the ship for home.

Our spirits lifted as we found the solution to each problem and the prospect of the long journey back assumed all the attraction of another adventure. The final decision now was what to take home and what to leave. We had arrived with little: the wedding presents were portable and mainly practical, with one disappointing exception. Michael Scott's office in Dublin was notable for searching out the latest and most stylish design of even the most common object. Our wedding present from my Modernist colleagues was a set of beautiful bowls, Italian design, made of metal and stove-enamelled matt black on the outside and brilliant primary colours on the inside. The trouble was that they had quickly rusted away in the African climate. We threw some of them out but kept a few – for sentiment. The biggest item we decided to take was a large cabinet I had designed to house our record player and LPs. I had this, together with a coffee table, made in the lovely mvule hardwood, so these were cherished. Nuala had bought a splendid Singer sewing machine and this joined other essential household items. We added our small collection of African crafts: beaded stools, drums, the Karamojong spear and other varied items, which some would call junk but to us had memories. An Asian trader offered to buy the remainder of the household furnishings, leaving us clear to make the final break.

I arranged to meet Walter one evening after work to discuss my possible move to join him in the Bachelors' Quarters and also to choose a room. I drove up the winding road to where the East Africa Company's compound was located, near the top of Kololo Hill. When I came around the final bend to the open space in front of the wide gates, I saw a scene of utter confusion. Cars were parked at every angle and people were running around, shouting and gesticulating. There were dozens of uniformed askaris and a small huddle of white people standing just inside the gate. I jumped out of the car and went through into the inner compound, to be accosted by an officious-sounding, white police officer.

'What are you doing here?'

'I'm meeting a friend, a resident.'

'What's his name?'

'Walter Ryder.'

There was a pause and the officer changed his tone. 'There's been an incident. I'm sorry to have to tell you that your friend has been killed. I have to go.'

He walked off, leaving me standing there, numb and speechless.

I went over to the little group of Europeans and asked them what had happened. Parker was not there and I did not know any of the others. They told me that they thought that Walter had been stabbed to death: this had apparently happened only about twenty minutes before and nobody knew who the killer was or why this horrible thing had occurred. There was a great deal of tension in the small group, and African workers and police stood well apart from the Europeans. The white officer suddenly came running out of the building, shouting orders to the askaris and then rushed over to our group. 'The killer is Jacob, the houseboy, and he has just run off. We must get him before he disappears into the forest. I want volunteers to drive my men in a search of the whole area.'

My mind was in turmoil but here was a call for action, at least of some sort. Hardly thinking, I instantly offered to join the hunt and the officer ordered two of his men into my car. All the cars raced off down the road to split in various directions for the search. The only scrap of information I had been hurriedly given was that Jacob, who was normally resident at the Bachelors' Quarters, had friends in Katwe. I headed there in growing darkness, now filled with a conviction that I was taking decisive action that would somehow make the fact of Walter's killing easier to bear. I drove down the winding road, far too fast and when tree trunks loomed in the headlights the tyres screamed, but all I could think about was that I must do something to help.

Katwe was in the lower part of the city: a chaotic unplanned shanty town which in happier times and daylight, seemed a quirky, cheerful place. Approaching the edge of the sprawling township in darkness revealed a different scene. There were no streetlamps: only the occasional flickering oil lamp spilled light out on to the beaten earth of the unpaved roads. These were a disordered tangle of unrelated tracks, bumpy and potholed and with dangerously deep storm drains to be avoided at every turn. I stopped the car and asked the askaris, 'Where do you think he might be?' They looked at me blankly and shook their heads. They had no idea, but one suggested that he might be drinking at one of the beer halls or shebeens and offered to guide me there. I was beginning to feel that we were lost in this maze of alleys and had a growing anxiety about the situation I was in. After a bewildering series of turns and reverses, the blank side wall of the hall was lit up in our headlights. It was a large corrugated iron roofed structure, crudely built of unplastered concrete blocks. We parked a little distance away and walked up to the open doorway. The interior was dimly lit with naked bulbs hanging from the rafters. There were maybe a couple of dozen men, some standing at a simple bar counter with the others sitting at trestle tables. Everybody looked up as we entered but nobody spoke. The thought that came to me was, 'What the hell am I doing here'.

I turned to the black policemen and saw unease if not fear in their faces and knew then that I had stupidly allowed myself to get involved in this manhunt. I was probably the only white person in Katwe at that moment and wanted to be as far away as possible.

Forcing myself to walk slowly, I turned and, followed by the two askaris, went back to the car: a distance that now seemed twice the length. When I was closing the driver's door,

I saw that a crowd had gathered at the hall entrance and was staring at us. My grief at the death of Walter was now paramount and I realized the futility of looking for revenge or retribution or whatever possessed me to engage in the madness of this senseless search. The streetlights were a huge relief after the threatening shadows, as we eventually bumped out on to the paved road. I dropped the two police back to the station and drove the long way back to Mbuya to give the awful news to Nuala. After the baby's death only a few months before, this double blow was almost too much to bear. We had now lost one of our closest friends. We wondered what was next?

The next morning the full story of the tragedy unfolded. It appeared that Jacob, a servant employed for a number of years in the East Africa Company premises, had accidentally knocked over a glass of water. Unfortunately, the glass contained Parker's false teeth and these were broken in the fall. The Kenyan was enraged when the houseboy told him about the mishap. He promptly sacked him, ordered him to get out at once and refused to pay him the week's wages he was due. Jacob left in tears, went down to Katwe where he quickly got extremely drunk. He came back to the quarters that afternoon to demand the money he was entitled to by law, only to find that Parker was not there. The theory then was that he picked up a kitchen knife and stabbed the first white man he came across. This happened to be Walter. The inexplicability of the act was hard to grasp: Walter was above all a kindly man, as far removed from the arrogant white settler type as could be. He was popular with the African servants, would joke and laugh with them and, above all, he was fair-minded.

The full horror of the story, however, did not end with Walter's death. In the early dawn they found Jacob. He was hanging from a tree at the edge of the forest. We asked John, our houseboy, why Jacob had done what he did? John shrugged in a matter-of-fact way.

'He had to,' he said. 'He had disgraced his family and his tribe.'

For some days Walter's murder chilled the small white community of Kampala. The killing of a European was an extremely rare event in Uganda, but the shadow of the horrific Mau Mau campaign and counter-campaign across the border in Kenya now seemed closer. There was a muted response, however, to any blame being based on race or colour and, if anything, the behaviour of Parker came in for the greatest condemnation, except, of course, in the usual hind-bound circles. I could not bear to speak to him or even to see him.

The morning of Walter's funeral brought another typical African day of endless blue skies and blazing sun. The large group that gathered at the roadside verge outside the cemetery was mainly white, with a scattering of Asians and Africans. The floral summer dresses of the women and the Sunday-style white shirts and shorts of the men belied the mournfulness of the occasion. It was, however, heartbreaking for Nuala and me to proceed up that path under the mimosas, which only a few months earlier we had walked with Walter and Niall's tiny casket. It was now Walter's coffin we closely followed up that same path to his freshly dug grave, only yards away from the still raw, earthen mound of our baby's plot. We stood there for the final prayers, remembering Walter's rich Scottish accent and his infectious laugh but now and then I could only look over at the little mvule cross, on which I had painted Niall's name in white, remembering also that heartrending day.

We gathered in small groups on the roadside verge before departure and the talk was stilted and inconsequential, but when I heard Parker's loud tone in one of his racist rants, I pushed my way in fury over to him and said, 'All this is your fault and you know it. I don't want to ever see your face again.'

I turned away from him and Nuala and I went back to where Sarah, who had been minding Eoin, was waiting in our car.

The time to say goodbye to our staff had come and to close up our house on Mbuya. Nuala had contacted Jean in Nairobi to say that she was on her way. John was philosophical about our departure. Most house servants were well used to the transient nature of employment in European households and knew he would get a good reference. Sarah was unhappy, however; she had become attached to little Eoin or '*Honi kidogo*' as she called him. Our shamba boy was shared with others and thus the consequence of our leaving was less onerous for him. The African bush telegraph had long signalled our going and we had a number of brief visits to say farewell. One of these, an irregular visitor and a person we always warmly welcomed, was a grey-haired *mzee* with a wonderfully wizened face. He would suddenly appear on our veranda, a long tattered overcoat over his grubby *kanzu*, offering a small bunch of sweet bananas for sale, all conducted in a most dignified manner. We always bought them from him, although every Saturday morning we also came back from the market with a huge bunch. A young Somali woman was another occasional door-to-door seller, this time of local crafts. She had long hair, tied back in a fashion that emphasized her high cheekbones: she was strikingly beautiful, her willowy figure clad in colourful material. Several of the neighbouring house servants also, somewhat shyly, said farewell when we met them on our track.

In the early afternoon of our last day in our house on Mbuya, a truck ground up the track to our veranda. At least a half-dozen cheerful and raggedly dressed men unloaded two wooden crates and began to pack the belongings we were shipping home. After a couple of hours of banter and high-pitched chatter and laughter, the crates were nailed up and, with rhythmic chants and whoops, the two containers were loaded into the back of the truck and the entourage drove off.

Nuala and Eoin left early the next morning to board the train for Nairobi. Most of our friends came to the platform to see them off and, although the gathering was generally light-hearted, there was, as always, the underlying lump-in-the-throat sadness about saying goodbye. I was now on my own and for the next few weeks or possibly months – I still did not know how long my work would last – I would have to cope. I had savagely turned my back on anything to do with Parker or his ilk, but Brian Kavanagh had come to the rescue and offered a place for me to stay at his school at Namilyango. I accepted his offer at once: it would be good for me to get out of Kampala and away, at least for some of the time, from the despondency of the past few months.

Namilyango College was about 12 miles from Kampala, off the road to Jinja and near the little village of Seta. For me, however, it seemed a million miles away from the misery of the past few months. It was a tranquil place: simple buildings with deep verandas and the gentle shade of acacias in open courtyards. I soon developed a steady pattern to my daily life which helped to pass those final lonely weeks and to dull, if not to ease, the sense of loss and disillusion. Brian told me a little of the history of the school. It had been founded in 1902. It was extraordinary that this was only twelve years after Stanley's last great expedition and a period of ferocious conflict and cruelty, both religious and internecine. It was difficult to imagine what it had been like in those days in the College's placid surroundings.

When I left for work each morning, the orange yellow glow of dawn was a brief drama, and the hanging gourds of what we called the 'sausage' trees were blackly silhouetted against the sky. Each evening, just before dark and retreat indoors from the inevitable insects, it was good to sit on a basket chair and listen to the sounds of the end of an African day: the rising chatter of cicadas; dogs barking; distant voices and laughter, and sometimes the sound of a far-off drum.

'SAUSAGE' TREE

CHAPTER 10

OUT OF AFRICA

Early one morning the axe finally fell.

I HAD BARELY SETTLED at my drawing board when the senior partner poked his head around the half-open door and asked would I come to his office. I knew what to expect and was not surprised when he launched into a long litany of problems that were inevitably going to affect the future of the practice; the slowing down of new commissions; difficulties of settlements of fees and, above all, the uncertainties about the imminent arrival of independence. He eventually came to the point: the staff numbers would have to be reduced and this would mean that some contracts might have to be, as he said, 'shortened'. What he really meant was terminated. He went on to say that since the original period of my contract was almost complete, the practice was willing to honour the full four months' paid home leave I would have been entitled to if I would agree to go earlier. He also said that, of course, I would be paid a bonus, as originally had been promised.

My mind had already been made up: I wanted to go, and as soon as possible. Back at my drawing board I surveyed the silent room. The two Sikhs had their heads down. Gurvinder always worked steadily and Chana was, as usual, stroking his beard. The place beside me was empty, the drawing board bare. I remembered what a cheerful place the office had been when Walter was there and smiled to myself when I recalled the 'day of the earthquake', and his gallows humour after that incident of just a few weeks past. There had been this sudden total stillness, as if everything had stopped, then an unearthly shudder with the steel windows rattling in the concrete frame of the building. It was over, almost before it started. Walter instantly announced it as an omen of doom and even the Sikhs laughed. I missed him now.

My departure was fixed for two weeks hence, to enable me to complete those projects of mine that were already at an advanced stage. I did not know how I would survive those next weeks: morale in the office was at its lowest, and walking past Mrs. Caffrey's scowling face at her desk each morning only multiplied the gloom. Help came from an unexpected source. One of our clients was an international oil company and its representative in Uganda called at the office to discuss the possibility of establishing a distribution depot in the far province of Kasese. He had arranged to travel out there and start negotiations to purchase a site, but was anxious to have an architect accompany him to advise him on suitable locations. Both partners were busy and it was suggested that I could go with him. I jumped at the chance: it would get me away from this doleful place, as well as offering the gift of another trip to that spectacular region, which was home to one of the finest wildlife reserves in East Africa and, best of all, the Mountains of the Moon.

I had already worked with the oil man, Rob Mindel, on

a number of small projects and we got on well. He had also known Walter from the sailing club. We started one morning from the office in his unwieldy-looking American car and set off to the west, the same route taken by Nuala and me in Walter's Citroën on our first adventure two years earlier. It was soon apparent that the Chevrolet was not built for the corrugations of Uganda's roads. The soft suspension set the car rolling and at one stage I thought that I would be seasick. It was also one of those short rainy seasons and between Masaka and Mbarara we went through deep floods where we had to have the usual help of cheerful African push crews. One of these pools was so much deeper that the car stalled and was too heavy to be pushed free. A helpful truck was standing by and towed us out – at a price.

We halted at that same high place that commanded a tremendous view out over the plain of the Queen Elizabeth Park and where I had imagined I could glimpse the snowfields of the Ruwenzori. The mountains were again true to their reputation: only menacing, purple black clouds filled the far horizon. The open flats below, however, were teeming with animals: antelope; wildebeest; buffalo and elephant, a herd of which crossed the road in front of us as we descended to the bridge over the Kazinga Channel. The only place to stay in this region was the Government Rest Camp and, exhausted after the long trip, we were glad to roll up to the entrance.

The next day we recrossed the Equator back north to the town of Kasese where the proposed oil depot was to be located. We spent a few hours here surveying several locations before returning to the camp in the early afternoon. Rob felt he needed a siesta, but I knew that these were my last days in

Uganda and had that familiar feeling of sadness at leaving places I might never see again. I went out with my camera to walk to the slight escarpment that overlooked the Channel. The stretch of short grass from the camp over to the water's edge was dotted with the candelabra-like euphorbia trees but looked clear of animal life. The waters below were filled with hippos and the sandy shores were crowded with white herons and storks. When I turned to go back to the camp, I saw to my horror that dozens of buffalo had strayed out and were now barring my direct route. Walking straight past them would not be a good idea. Instead I slowly worked my away along the banks of the Channel, keeping in the cover of euphorbias to circle around the herd. I did get good photographs, but Rob told me that I should have known better.

Nuala and I had made tentative plans for our departure but now firm dates and bookings would have to be finalized: the most important being the date of sailing from Mombasa. I confirmed this with the shipping agents, allowing a generous amount of time for a stay in Kenya and a roundabout sightseeing trip to the coast. Our boxed possessions were consigned separately and would not arrive home for several months.

My final day at work came at last. There was no farewell ceremony, no party, just handshakes from the partners and from the rest of the staff. The senior partner handed me my cheque, which included, I was told, my bonus. This was a good deal less than I had expected. When I queried the amount, he rambled apologetically about hard times and difficult conditions but all I wanted to do was to get away and left quickly, with little regret. Before I went to bed that night at Namilyango I went outside to look up at the sky, that always-predictable African night sky, a coruscation of stars in an eternity of inky black. I tried to identify some of the constellations and stars but, except for a splendidly sparkling Orion, I could name no others. This was not always so. I was a boy in the years of World War II when my father acquired an ancient encyclopaedia that contained a splendid pull-out map of the stars. I remembered now several of those names – Cassiopeia, Betelgeuse, Andromeda and Pegasus – and how I learned to pick them out in the night skies of home where a clear starlight display was rare and unpredictable. I was in a mix of emotions – homesick, on the one hand: I longed to see again the wild Atlantic from a western headland or storm clouds racing past a gibbous moon – but, staring up now at the vast arching heavens, the essential stillness of Africa again ensnared me.

I left early to arrive at the bank just at opening time. It would be a very long drive to Nairobi, two days at least, and I was anxious not to have to drive at night: the Emergency – as it was called – was still in force in Kenya and I did not want to be caught out in darkness. I needed to cash part of the cheque for the long journey home and transfer the rest into an account of our own. I handed it in at the counter and when the teller looked at it he said, 'Please wait a moment' and disappeared into an inner office. I was not particularly bothered since the amount was probably larger than usually presented by most individuals. After an exceptionally long wait, another, obviously more senior, official came over to me and announced, in a low voice, that he was sorry but that they were not in a position to honour the cheque. I was dumbfounded. How could this be, I said? 'Insufficient funds' was the answer. 'What else can go wrong?' I asked myself, in a mixture of despair and anger. My immediate reaction was to return to the firm and demand an explanation, but after reflection I tried to think of a different solution. I phoned Rob, my friend from the previous week's adventure and told him of my problem. I knew that his company owed the firm for design work that had recently been billed to them. He was instantly supportive and concerned at the way I had been treated and said that he would come to the bank and do what he could to help.

I waited in the reception area for an anxious hour, brooding on my precarious situation. The cost of Nuala's return fare, as well as the shipping of our car and possessions, had already come from our own pockets and we would need all the money I had earned to survive until I could get another job. The prospect of being stranded in Africa, almost penniless, was not a pleasant one. When Rob arrived, he was ushered into the manager's office and there was another wait to be endured. After about a half hour Rob emerged, still chatting to the manager, who then called me over and asked me, 'What way do you want us to deal with your cheque?' I told him that I wanted the bulk of the money to be transferred to an account in Barclays Bank in London, with the remainder in cash for our journey home. The various papers were signed and when the business was concluded, I thanked Rob warmly and we said our goodbyes. I drove out on to the Jinja road, not wanting to pass by the office on Grant Street: that part of my life was over and I was still angry at the long delay in honouring their cheque. It was, however, a huge relief to feel financially secure, at least for the near future.

The cemetery was at the edge of the city. I stopped the car at the entrance and sat for a long while, my mind a tangle of emotions. It was hard to start the walk up the path to the two mounds near the rear boundary, where grass was now covering the raw earth. Walter's grave remained unmarked, but the little wooden cross with the name 'Niall' picked out in white stood straight. It was harder still to turn away. I stood for a while and looked around me: overhead the feathery foliage of the mimosas whispered in a gentle breeze and the old weathered red-brick wall at the rear was draped with fronds of bougainvillea. It was a tranquil place. I had to leave but to turn my back and walk away was as heartbreaking as those awful days not long past.

I drove off but the sense of abandoning was now added to the pain of loss and for many miles on that long road to the east I could still feel the pull of this emotion.

I crossed the Nile at the Owen Falls Dam and left the last stretch of surfaced road. It would be red murram and corrugations now for most of the way to Nairobi and indeed practically all the way to the Indian Ocean. When the great mass of Mount Elgon appeared in front, I finally left Uganda and entered Kenya at the tiny border post of Malaba. After that late start and my slow progress on bad roads, I thought I would be lucky to make the 250 miles in daylight to Eldoret, where I hoped to spend the night. The road improved a little after I passed the Nandi Escarpment and just before dusk the straggling settlement appeared. The Royal East African Association Handbook numbered the population as 8, 193, of whom 888 were European. The map, however, displayed a place parcelled out by race. The 'Native Location' was tucked behind the industrial area, with the Eldoret West Estate described as 'Asian'. The main area of the map was then, presumably white, or perhaps I should say, European.

The hotel gave me a room and directed me to the dining room and bar. This was a high-roofed, pleasant space with a veranda facing the street and, unmistakably, it was a micro-cosm of the White Highlands. The bar was fairly crowded and every person was white, except for the staff. I sat at a table near the bar and observed the goings-on. There was a fairly even mixture of men and women; the men were uniformly dressed in khaki bush shirts with shorts or slacks and all wore wide-brimmed hats, most with leopard skin bands. Many of the women were similarly clad, although a few wore dresses – the flowery, summer style that were no different to those invariably worn by white women in Kampala. It was the guns that shocked me first and almost everyone seemed to have one, the women as well as the men. Handguns in leather holsters hung from belts and there was an air of swaggering arrogance far removed from the Africa of my experience.

One figure stood out from the rest of this somewhat raucous and ill-dressed crowd. She sat on a bar stool, dressed in smart jodhpurs with highly polished boots. Her open-necked shirt was dazzling white and she had a small silk neckerchief knotted around her throat. She also had a broad-brimmed hat, but this was thrown back, releasing her long auburn hair. The finishing touch had to be the small pearl-handled revolver in a dainty holster attached to her belt: a fashion decoration, perhaps, rather than a menacing weapon. Men admirers surrounded her and her stylish femininity was a definite contrast to the otherwise overwhelming male aggressiveness that pervaded the place.

I slept late, exhausted after the gruelling drive and then my start was further delayed by a long wait in the local garage to have the car checked. It was over 200 miles to Nairobi, across the Great Rift Valley and then the climb up to the plateau and high country of Kenya. This entire region was Kikuyu-land, but also the main White Highlands, and it was here that most of the violence of the past six years had devastated this beautiful and bountiful land. Although the worst of the turmoil had ebbed, I did not want to be still on the road after dark.

I had started in Kampala at an altitude of 4,000 feet and the road to Nairobi went up to 9,000 feet. My motoring handbook had warned of possible difficulties in driving from lowlands to high altitudes and when the Fiat began to struggle on the first of the steep ascents to the plateau, I took heed and stopped at intervals to give the engine a rest: there was also the usual problem of the water pump and the need to refill the radiator. All this took time and it was getting dark long before I reached the last of the steep climbs. Then, suddenly, I felt the engine power slipping away and the car stalled. Fortunately, I had managed to steer it into the side of the road but it was pitch dark and there was no traffic.

I had never felt more alone. I sat for a while before summoning up the courage to get out and see if I could solve the problem. The silence was palpable, but then I heard the faint bubbling of an overheating radiator and hoped that that was just the problem. Let everything cool and then, with luck, top up and start again. I consoled myself thus and settled in for a long wait. Nothing stirred outside, no vehicle passed, thoughts of the Mau Mau came and faded. I forced myself to let an hour pass before carefully and slowly filling up the radiator with the spare water. After a couple of false starts, the engine fired and soon the steep climb was over and the far glow of the lights of Nairobi was a huge relief.

It was late and I had some difficulty finding Philip and Jean's house but when I arrived Nuala was still up and waiting for me. After the past few months of loneliness and growing alienation from my circumstances, it was good to warmly embrace and feel part of a family again. Eoin was fast asleep, having been expecting me all day and asking when Daddy would come. We then made the mistake of waking him and, as a result, he stayed wide awake all night: he shared the bedroom with us and our celebrations for my return had to be constrained.

We explored a little of the city the next morning and, straying off one of the main streets, found ourselves facing a grim reminder of this so-called 'Emergency'. A high, iron mesh fence, topped with barbed wire, lined one side of the road, forming the front of an enormous open cage. Inside the enclosure were several hundred black Africans, some standing, others squatting with fingers clutching the mesh barrier. It was an unnerving sight, and we felt ashamed and guilty to stare from the outside of this obscenity and, worse still, to be

stared at by those caged: impassive stares that spoke of discon-
nection – an unbridgeable gulf. It was a detention centre, we
were told later, one of many. where anyone who could be
suspected or denounced as a possible supporter of the Mau
Mau could be rounded up, interrogated and either released or
sent on to one of the huge prisons. The innocent as well as the
guilty could be caught up in the sweeps that were now seen
by some as draconian and even brutal. Many of the white
settlers, however, rejoiced at the measures and there were
many Parkers in Kenya who wanted white rule to prevail and
the harshest measures to continue. Gruesome judicial
hangings were often the response and some of the more
extreme white settlers demanded that these be public execu-
tions, 'to teach them a lesson', as I heard one person say.

It was another Kenya that the four of us, now accompanied
by two small boys, set out to experience at the weekend. The
area of the Rift Valley just north of Nairobi was now considered safe to visit, at least in daylight hours. Our goal was to
see Lake Nakuru, the home of the famous flamingoes. The
Great Rift Valley stretched from the barren, semi-desert
northern Kenya territory down to the plains of Tanganyika.
I had travelled part of this road on my night drive and it all
looked and felt so different now on a splendid morning of
sunshine. Not far outside the city the view from the escarpment was quintessential Africa, reminding Nuala and me of
that unforgettable panorama of the volcanoes in the Congo.
A smoky heat haze out over the vast plains to the west
softened the edges of distant hills, and blurred the horizon to
an infinity of space.

This entire region was volcanic, with Mount Longonot, an extinct or maybe just dormant volcano, dominating the near distance. The appropriately named Hell's Gate was close and we deviated to explore this strange geological world. After the pervasive greens of Uganda, the yellow ochre, red-streaked rocks, surrounding the hot bubbling mud ponds, were a rare and exciting spectacle. A perpetual cloud of steam hung overhead and it was easy to wonder if a cataclysmic eruption might happen at any time.

The vast estate of Lord Delamere once ranged over the area surrounding the beautiful fresh water Lake Naivasha. In the 1930s this was the home of the infamous 'Happy Valley' set, a decadent colonial autocracy. It was still white settler country and, no wonder, with its fertile land and almost perfect climate at 6,000 feet. The Aberdare hills and forest were also close and these names often featured in news reports of the Mau Mau rebellion. The high forests were first the headquarters and then later the last refuges of fighters in the campaign which had ended in surrender just four years earlier. The green hills looked so peaceful now as we drove on to the fabled Lake Nakuru.

We bumped over a narrow track to a slight rise to see the wide expanse of shallow alkaline water and the extraordinary pageant of flamingoes. It looked as if there were hundreds of thousands of them, a constantly moving mass of swaying tall necks, pink and white plumage and spindly legs: a ballet as gracious as any devised by humans.

It was time to go. We were booked to sail from Mombasa in a week's time and our plan was to set out on one last trip, a

LAKE NAIVASHA

farewell to Africa safari. Our feelings were mixed: at one level we longed for home and to rebuild our lives, but at another level it was hard to leave this place of gargantuan skies and far-stretching distances. Those endless blue skies would be missed.

The problem of loading the car for the long expedition to the coast had first to be faced. Nuala had already taken some of our essential luggage on the train to Nairobi and I had almost filled the car for the drive from Kampala: there was now hardly an inch to spare. The solution was obvious – a roof rack – and a suitable one was quickly located and bolted into position. We loaded up the excess cases on top, stuffed the boot to capacity, squeezed the spare water can in front of the passenger seat and, with Eoin somewhat squashed between piled baggage, were enormously pleased at our ingenuity.

The plan was to head south for the Tanganyika frontier and Kilimanjaro, then, part circling that great mountain, turn east for the coast: a distance of nearly 500 miles, on mostly unsurfaced roads. We were not daunted. The Fiat had always managed to take us to the wilderness and back and we were sure it would not fail us now.

Barely a few miles outside Nairobi we detoured to explore the National Park and wildlife reserve. After our past years in East Africa, I suppose we had become blasé about encounters with wild animals, but it was still exhilarating to pause and watch a magnificent giraffe, neck stretched to reach the canopy of an acacia. The herds of gazelle, eland, waterbuck, zebra and buffalo were all familiar but it was the lions we were searching for. We had been told where to find them and sure enough there they were. A thicket of bushes were overshadowed by a few tall trees and in the deepest shade, quite close to the track, we could just make out the tawny forms that merged with the deep yellow grass. We cautiously drove nearer until we were almost on top of the group, but there was little stir from the lazily slumped great cats. Before we bumped out on to the roadway, we spotted a solitary rhino, standing still under a tree, a disconsolate-looking primordial creature.

It was here that the roof rack came apart for the first and

not the last time. A particularly savage pothole was the cause, the result being an explosion of suitcases and scattered contents all over the road. Eoin thought that this was a great joke, but we were not so happy. It took a while to collect all the items and tie up the cases with more of my cut-up climbing rope, which I had used to secure the cases on top. It happened twice more before we reached the border of Tanganyika and the only solution was to drive with extra caution, avoiding the deeper holes. By the time the shining snows of Kilimanjaro filled the horizon in front, we were ready to halt and a convenient rest camp provided a haven for the night.

Before we crossed the border at Namanga, it was tempting to visit the newly established Amboseli reserve. We had stopped to enjoy the sight of several ostriches striding past, with a whole flock of tiny fledglings tearing along to catch up when there was a heavy bump, and a baboon was staring at us through the windscreen. Several others joined him while the first one took hold of the wipers as if to dare us to stop him. They quickly got bored and jumped off, and we were able to move away over the wide savannah, with the great mountain a dazzling backdrop.

A few miles into Tanganyika the extinct volcano, Mount Meru, loomed ahead, although, when we drew nearer, its elegant 15,000-foot cone was dwarfed by the mass of Kilimanjaro. The landscape around the pretty little town of Arusha, up in this high mountain country, was lushly green, and it seemed like a good place to halt. There were still several hours of daylight left, however, and when I checked the distances given in the motoring handbook it seemed a better idea to

KILIMANJARO

push on 50 miles to the town of Moshi. This was at the foot
of the big mountain and it left us with one, albeit long, day's
journey to the coast. The whole area is the home of the
Chagga people and vast coffee plantations that roll in every
direction across gently rounded hills.

I walked out on to the veranda of the simple rest camp
that night and looked up at the darkening sky: our last night,
perhaps, in the highlands of Africa. I remembered some of

those other memorable nights; the frosty starlight above the rock overhangs of Kabamba in the high Ruwenzori; the warm velvet darkness over the plains of Karamoja and those far-off sounds, the essence of Africa, on my last night in Uganda.

Kilimanjaro, Africa's highest mountain at over 19,000 feet, rose splendidly alone, straight out of the high plains that surrounded it. The twin summits of Kibo and Mawenzi were sharply clear in the early morning light as we set out on our last day. Kibo's snows were blinding white in contrast to the black rocky pinnacles of Mawenzi, but when we turned off the main road to drive up to the tiny village of Marangu, our view of the summits was swallowed in the dense rain forest of the lower slopes. At the road head we were curious to see if we could find a better view of the snow peak by walking a short way up the track that led towards the summits. Eoin was quite capable of trotting along with us, but it was soon obvious that there would be hours of walking before the forest would relent. We turned back and resumed the last long leg to the sea.

We were barely back on the main road and only a few miles from re-entering Kenya when the roof rack suddenly slid down the side of the car and I almost lurched into the ditch. This was the last straw, I said, and viciously tore the rack and luggage off the car, ripped off the loose lashings and in a rage flung the twisted metal into the bushes at the side of the road. When I calmed down – Eoin again thought it was all a joke – Nuala helped me take each fallen piece of luggage and try to stow it on the already packed rear seats. With careful rearranging we managed to stow each item somewhere but now Eoin was perched high up on the extra luggage, quite happy with his enhanced view.

On an empty stretch of road and well over the Kenya frontier we stopped to allow the engine to cool and also to stretch our legs. A solitary flame tree partly framed a distant view of Kilimanjaro: the riotous clusters of scarlet blossoms were set against the yellow grass plains that stretched to the far-off white snows of the mountain. With the overarching blue sky, this was an enduring image of highland Africa, a land of primary colours, and one that we could never forget.

After the little settlement of Voi, we left the high country behind and started the long downhill road to the coast, the final 100 miles. When the first sliver of darkest blue formed the horizon, we knew that our safari was ending: the Indian Ocean at last and our first sight of the sea in almost three years. The Makapu causeway led us over the lagoon and on to the island of Mombasa where the bizarre twin archways of giant metal intertwined tusks formed a gateway to Kilindini Road and the Old Town. We were all exhausted and retired to bed early, hardly noticing the scruffy and run-down interior of our hotel. After the restful cool nights of the highlands, the awful heat and humidity gave us a horrible time of twisting and turning, our bodies slick with sweat. The mosquito nets were claustrophobic and mesh screens on the windows killed any hope of relief from a cross breeze. We must have finally slept for the relative cool of the early morning saw us freshly energized and eager to explore this ancient place.

The network of narrow streets, alleyways, white domes and minarets of mosques spoke more of the Middle East than of Africa and, to us, were a complete contrast to the brash uniformity of the newly built settlements inland. Mombasa had been founded by Arab traders almost a thousand years before and no doubt had been used as a staging post for slave trading raids into the interior for many of those years and certainly up to the times of Stanley, Burton and Dr. Livingstone. Our first desire, however, with the heat and humidity already building up, was to get to a beach and plunge into the salt waters. Nyali was the nearest one, we were told, and the sight of the unspoiled stretch of dazzling white sand, beyond a fringe of graceful palm trees, was enough to have us racing for our first dip. The reality was far from the fantasy: the sand was burning hot, and the sea, a long lagoon, was more like a hot bath.

It was cooler in the late afternoon when we explored deeper in the Old Town. The narrow alleyways were shaded, with the elaborate ornamental iron balconies and fretted shuttered windows adding to the place's mystery and intrigue. We eventually found our way up to Fort Jesus. This massive piece of military architecture was built by the Portuguese in the late sixteenth century and had been the focus of conflicts and sieges for nearly 300 years. The impressive, sharply angled bastions towered above us as we approached the gate, hoping to be allowed to have a stroll inside and a view from the top of the high walls. A heavily barred doorway faced us and while we stood there, wondering where a doorbell might be, a uniformed askari appeared behind the bars. He looked at us silently and I asked if we might be allowed to have a look inside. No answer. After a few moments another figure appeared and asked what we wanted. 'We are interested in the building and wondered if we could have a look inside'. 'This is a prison', he replied.

FORT JESUS, MOMBASA

We walked slowly away, trying not to look foolish or so naïve as, no doubt, the prison guards thought we were. I had a last look up at one of the bastions and saw faces staring from a barred embrasure.

The old harbour was filled with dhows and must have looked like this as far back as the time of those early Arab traders and certainly when the great explorer Vasco da Gama called here in 1498. The design of the shapely craft with their lovely pointed prows and high sterns had hardly changed over the centuries. These vessels, as well as provisioning the settlement from Arabia, exported ivory and the unfortunate, manacled, black slaves from the interior, most sold by their mercenary-minded chiefs and kings.

The day of our departure came at last. We drove to the new harbour to see our ship, which had arrived in the night from the Cape. She was the *SS Kenya*, a slender, white-painted liner with coloured bunting fluttering from the masts. This ship and her sister vessel, the *SS Uganda*, continuously served the route from Cape Town to the Port of London. Our route would be up the Gulf of Aden, through the Red Sea and the Suez Canal, then across the Mediterranean, Gibraltar and on up the Bay of Biscay. We were to call at Aden, Port Said, Malta and Barcelona. All this was relayed to us at the shipping office and, to us, was a hugely exciting prospect of adventure.

It was time to embark, but first we had to wait and see our car being hoisted aboard. When our turn came, we watched in some apprehension as the slings were tightened and the little Fiat was hoisted high and then swung over the deck, to be lowered into the hold. We climbed the gangway and the purser showed us to our cabin, our home for the next three weeks.

The ship's siren blared and a great burst of martial music poured out from the tannoys. We were standing on deck and our neighbour told us that the captain was an ex-Royal Navy man who liked to keep up his old traditions. To the loud strains of Colonel Bogey's march, we watched the ropes being cast off and now the passengers on deck flung multi-coloured paper streamers down to the dockside crowd, waving farewell. More streamers were thrown back from the land until the whole side of the ship was covered in a kaleidoscope of dancing colour. After the ship moved away from the quay, the connections were broken and when the streamers now trailed in the water, the figures on the land dwindled.

Out in the open Indian Ocean, we walked to the stern and, holding Eoin up to the rail, stared back over the frothing wake. I could still feel the pull of Africa for a long while as the distant shoreline melted into the haze of approaching night.